Transforming the Business of Government: Insights on Resiliency, Innovation, and Performance

Transforming the Business of Government: Insights on Resiliency, Innovation, and Performance

Edited by

Daniel J. Chenok and Michael J. Keegan

IBM Center for The Business of Government

ROWMAN & LITTLEFIELD PUBLISHERS, INC.

Lanham • Boulder • New York • London

ROWMAN & LITTLEFIELD PUBLISHERS, INC.

Published in the United States of America
by Rowman & Littlefield Publishers, Inc.
A wholly owned subsidiary of The Rowman & Littlefield Publishing Group, Inc.
4501 Forbes Boulevard, Suite 200, Lanham, Maryland 20706
www.rowmanlittlefield.com

Unit A, Whitacre Mews, 26-34 Stannary Street, London SE11 4AB

Copyright © 2024 by IBM Center for The Business of Government

British Library Cataloguing in Publication Information Available

Library of Congress Cataloging-in-Publication Information has been requested

ISBN 9781538193457 (Hardcover)
ISBN 9781538193464 (Paperback)
ISBN 9781538193471 (Ebook)

Printed in the United States of America

∞™ The paper used in this publication meets the minimum requirements of American
National Standard for Information Sciences—Permanence of Paper for Printed Library
Materials, ANSI/NISO Z39.48-1992.

TABLE OF CONTENTS

INTRODUCTION: TWENTY-FIVE YEARS OF CONNECTING RESEARCH TO PRACTICE

By Daniel J. Chenok and Michael J. Keegan

INTRODUCTION

Governments face increasingly serious, seemingly intractable public management challenges that go to the core of effective governance and leadership, testing the very form, structure, and capacity required to meet and overcome such challenges. Many problems facing public sector leaders are wickedly complex, do not respect bureaucratic boundaries, and are nonlinear and fluid in nature, "where very small effects may produce disproportionate impacts."[1] In many ways, traditional government approaches seem obsolete and incapable of meeting evolving complexity.[2] Prescriptions abound on how best to address these issues, coalescing around calls for whole of government, enterprise,[3] and networked[4] approaches.

Moreover, government leaders continue to face the unforgiving realities of disruption and uncertainty. Agency officials increasingly indicate that what were previously viewed as Black Swan events are now becoming more frequent—and more destabilizing.[5] The vulnerability of social and economic well-being is magnified by reliance on both connectivity and distributed value chains subject to disruption on multiple fronts. Risks have grown due to complex variables such as geopolitical conflicts, multiple public health emergencies, and natural disasters (e.g., wildfires, hurricanes, drought). Addressing risks has placed renewed emphasis on the importance of being resilient. The combination of perpetual uncertainty and an ever-evolving risk environment continuously overtakes current planning models.

Given this new reality, government leaders need practical, actionable insights on how best to manage and lead through uncertain and disruptive periods. For 25 years, the IBM Center for The Business of Government has sought to inform government leaders and stakeholders by supporting independent research from recognized public management experts, with the overarching goal of improving public sector management and operations. The Center's collaboration with scholars, thought leaders, and government executives intends to spark the imagination—identifying emerging trends, original ideas, and best practices, and providing decision makers with knowledge about the benefits and challenges of transformation. The Center delivers on this mission by publishing first-class research that provides lessons learned and insights to better address mission and management challenges in an increasingly uncertain world.

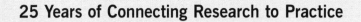

25 Years of Connecting Research to Practice

❝ *Unlike traditional scholarly outlets, the IBM Center makes explicitly clear that its reports are to be 'written for government executives and managers' and that in making the decision to fund research proposals, it looks for very practical findings and recommendations—not just theory and concepts—in order to assist executives and managers to more effectively respond to mission and management challenges.* **❞**

Source: Journal of Public Administration Research and Theory (2010) 21 (suppl 1): pp. i99-i112. Minnowbrook III: A special issue.

From Mission and Management Challenges to Preparing for Uncertainty

The IBM Center released its latest research agenda to meet current mission and management challenges facing frontline government executives. The Center has also dedicated time and resources to explore how best government agencies can prepare, address, and overcome the disruptive inevitabilities of "future shocks"—those increasingly common and severe events that have effects within and across nations.

Partnering with the National Academy of Public Administration (Academy) and the IBM Institute for Business Value, as well as other U.S. and global partners, the Center launched a "Future Shocks" initiative in 2022 to help government leaders further identify core capabilities critical to building resilience, building on lessons learned from pandemic response efforts. Governments, around the world have navigated and responded to the impacts of the pandemic, and have captured valuable lessons and gained an understanding of critical areas of focus. The Future Shocks initiative sparked a series of international roundtable discussions with global leaders from across the public, private, academic, and nonprofit sectors to capture lessons learned, share insights, and offer guidance in several core areas:

- Emergency preparedness and response

- Cybersecurity

- Supply chain

- Sustainability

- Workforce

In each of these areas, insights from these roundtables were documented in a series of published reports that offer strategies and actions to help governments address challenges that lie ahead. These roundtables and reports leveraged previous work that build on past experiences, such as a series of IBM Center reports on pandemic response, along with IBV studies and the Academy's Grand Challenges effort.[6] Insights derived from the Future Shocks series and reports inform the first six chapters of this book.

Leveraging Innovation and Performance to Drive Government Forward

To commemorate our 25th anniversary and identify innovative ideas that help government move forward in the face of inevitable uncertainty, the Center conducted a Challenge grant competition. This competition solicited essays from academics and thought leaders describing a future of government that can help inform agency readiness—identifying strategic actions for innovation and performance to drive agency missions forward. These essays pointed to new ways of understanding and framing problems; new processes to solve problems; and new implementation solutions. The essays, featured in the second half of this book, focus on a handful of specific topics:

- **Intelligent automation (IA), including artificial intelligence (AI),** is revolutionizing how governments derive value and insights from data to achieve key goals and objectives. An effective automation program can greatly enhance the ability of the public sector to improve services. The challenge going forward is to design and implement IA and AI programs with critical elements to successfully enable mission delivery and citizen services.

- **Data and evidence** can help government executives and managers to do more of what works to deliver better outcomes. This challenges leaders to collect accurate and timely data, conduct more informed analysis, make better decisions, and take smarter actions. Governments must also seek high-quality data to derive insights for improved delivery.

- **Shared services** in the federal government have focused primarily on "back office" functions of financial management, human resources, acquisition, and technology related functions. More recently, grants and cybersecurity services have been added to human resource and finance as the focus of dedicated Quality Service Management Offices (QSMOs). Shared platforms across open ecosystems can enable agencies to leverage innovative and cost-effective services, both to modernize the scope of existing services and develop new ones.

- **Customer experience** is now a key strategic priority across federal agencies. Focusing on customer experience (CX) enables agencies to improve service and build trust. By delivering a great experience for customers, agencies can provide great value for the people they serve. CX thus becomes a strategic imperative in mission delivery, and a foundational element for trust in government. Optimizing new technologies can enhance the user experience and incentivize innovators to modernize how government does business and delivers services.

Nine essays—encompassing such topics as AI, quantum computing, data and evidence, oversight, shared services, and customer experience—comprise Part III, chapters 7-15 of this book.

Guide to Reading Transforming the Business of Government

Part I. Roadmaps To Government Resiliency

Resilience involves more than pushing through after adversity or disappointment—but rather, resilient organizations turn crisis into opportunity and discover value in the unexpected. *Anticipating the future*—getting ahead of events rather than being subsumed by them—becomes integral to positioning, resourcing, and preparing an agency for what may come, while always keeping focus on primary mission responsibilities.

As outlined below, the chapters in Part I of this book offer insights and recommendations for government leaders and stakeholders on how best to discover value in the unexpected, and in doing so to more effectively position and lead organizations in the face of the unknown.

Chapter One—Emergency Preparedness and Response. This chapter focuses on the complex and crosscutting nature of disasters that do not respect geography, jurisdiction, political, or organizational boundaries. Emergency management should follow suit, recognizing that a key to success is the strength of networks that enable collaboration before, during, and after a disaster. This chapter reflects on what governments can do in the near term to better prepare and respond to exigent situations, identifying six recommendations and a host of associated action steps.

Chapter Two—Cybersecurity. This chapter examines today's complex cyber threat environment, and the government's responsibility to secure a safe and secure digital ecosystem. It focuses how best to reduce the impact of cyber incidents by developing and implementing strategies that promote resilience through public-private partnerships. The chapter offers a series of actions designed to help governments emerge stronger from current and future cyber shocks.

Chapter Three—Supply Chain. This chapter explores the role that governments play in preparing for supply chain disruptions. It assesses how governments can foresee potential challenges, plan responses ahead of time, and be ready to minimize the impacts of supply chain disruptions. The chapter outlines insights and recommendations on how best to diagnose threats, design responses, and sustain supply chains.

Chapter Four—Sustainability. This chapter spotlights the critical importance of integrating sustainability and climate resilience strategies into government institutions as climate impacts continue to mount. It focuses on key issues that include a clean energy transition, sustainable development, and water management, and offers practical insights and recommended actions that governments can take to build climate resilience.

Chapter Five—Workforce. This chapter points out that the public sector's traditional standardized approaches to recruiting, hiring, developing, and retaining talent no longer meet current and emerging needs. It offers insights and recommendations that governments can take to create and sustain workforces needed to address current and future systemic shocks.

Part II. Building Resilience: Preparation and Response

The unprecedented number and scope of catastrophic events stress governments, businesses, communities, and individuals. These cascading, disruptive events have raised fundamental questions about what capacities governments need to anticipate, prepare for, and respond to crises.

In **Chapter Six—*Eight Areas for Government Action*** summarizes key capabilities needed to address shocks, identifying recommended actions in eight capability areas that governments can take to anticipate, prepare for, and respond to new challenges that will continually arise. The underlying capacity of governments needs to be significantly augmented across these eight actions in two interrelated ways:

- Improve working relationships and alignment among network partners in governments, the private sector, civil society, and the public.

- Strengthen capabilities to operate successfully in a networked environment.

The overarching goal of building these capabilities is to help governments become more resilient in the face of inevitable future shocks.

Part III. On Future Readiness: Insights From Experts

Part III introduces compelling insights and timely perspectives from academics and practitioners on a variety of topics that can help governments address evolving future shocks and other scenarios. These nine chapters address larger themes of *innovation* and *performance*, to assist government leaders in efforts to enhance agency readiness. Each chapter outlines specific topics, capabilities, skills, technologies, and paths forward. The chapters encompass topics as diverse as AI, quantum computing, data and evidence, oversight, shared services, and customer experience.

Innovation

Chapter Seven—AI Literacy: A Prerequisite for the Future of AI and Automation in Government. This chapter outlines a three-phased approach for boosting AI literacy, presenting key actions and practices to make government organizations more responsive in delivering exceptional public services and achieve mission success.

Chapter Eight—Design Principles for Responsible Use of AI to Enhance CX Through Public Procurement. This chapter delves into the elements of service delivery, including the systems, people, and processes that indirectly influence customer experience (CX). It proposes two ways that public procurement processes can improve CX through artificial intelligence, and presents seven design principles to guide the procurement of AI tools in the public sector.

Chapter Nine—The Quantum Technology Challenge: What Role for the Government? This chapter discusses quantum technology, examining the impact on cybersecurity and cryptography as well as how quantum might impact environmental sustainability and labor. The last sections of the chapter focus on effective government strategies to make the best use of this emerging technology.

Chapter Ten—Using Linked Administrative Data to Advance Evidence-Based Policymaking. This chapter explores how to improve the use of existing administrative data based on a case study of a Statewide Longitudinal Data System (SLDS). SLDS can break down silos within government, facilitate shared governance, and answer research questions between state partners, while highlighting the benefits of data driven decision making. The use of SLDS data is transforming evidence-based policymaking, providing a model for how states and other governmental entities can better leverage administrative data for a broader set of purposes.

Performance

Chapter Eleven—Toward More Useful Federal Oversight. This chapter recognizes that federal oversight can be made more useful to more users for more purposes. Continually evolving technologies make it easier and more affordable to collect, analyze, and use oversight data and analyses to anticipate, detect, prepare for, prevent, and respond to problems more quickly, fully, and successfully. It seeks to engage others in acting to adopt more useful approaches to oversight that improve government performance on multiple dimensions.

Chapter Twelve—The Future of Payment Integrity within the U.S. Federal Government. This chapter outlines a vision that empowers agencies and federally funded programs, including state administered programs, to use data proactively in promoting payment integrity—transforming the identification, prevention, and recovery of improper payments and mitigating the effects of fraud. It emphasizes a pivot from compliance to prevention-focused strategies, promoting the use of data and analytics and collaboration across government and the private commercial sectors.

Chapter Thirteen—Leveraging Inspectors General to Make Evidenced-Based Decisions. This chapter examines the role of Offices of Inspectors General (OIGs), describes the concept of agile oversight, and provides examples of how OIGs can drive greater value.

Chapter Fourteen—A "One Agency" Approach to Enhanced Mission Enabling Services. This chapter explores NASA's approach to mission enablement services, illustrating a proven example of the "one firm" mindset and approach that can be adapted by government agencies. It offers recommendations and considerations to move shared services forward in the federal government.

Chapter Fifteen—Building and Maintaining Customer Trust in Government Services. This chapter describes how the ongoing evolution of government customer experience efforts can ultimately succeed, and makes a series of predictions on areas where customer experience for agencies may face the most significant challenges over the next few decades.

LOOKING FORWARD

The 21st century experience has provided lessons on the power of the unexpected. Yet systems in place to meet anticipated problems have often fallen short in meeting novel challenges. Uncertainty remains constant, despite collective efforts to ameliorate the tension between ongoing operations and inevitable disruptions.

As one expert observer has noted:

> Longing to reduce uncertainty and doubt has driven much of our progress. The more we noticed, remembered, wrote down, and shared, the more knowledgeable we became and the better we were to pass our learning on for future generations to increase.[7]

With this disclaimer that no one can know for certain what may come next, the insights and actions detailed in this book provide a practical path forward in transforming the business of government to meet evolving demands.

Daniel J. Chenok is Executive Director of the IBM Center for The Business of Government.

Michael J. Keegan is the Leadership Fellow at the IBM Center for The Business of Government and Host of The Business of Government Hour.

Endnotes

1   Heffernan, Margaret, *Uncharted: How to Map the Future*, Avid Reader Press, New York, NY, 2020, xiii.

2   Kettl, Donald, *Reflections on 21st Century Government Management*, IBM Center for The Business of Government, Washington, D.C. 2007, https://www.businessofgovernment.org/sites/default/files/KettlKelmanReport.pdf.

3   *Tackling Wicked Government Problems: A Practical Guide for Developing Enterprise Leaders*, edited by Jackson Nickerson and Ronald Sanders, Brookings Institution Press, Washington, D.C., 2013.

4   DeSeve, G. Edward, *Managing Recovery: An Insider's View*, IBM Center for The Business of Government, Washington D.C., 2011, https://www.businessofgovernment.org/sites/default/files/Managing%20Recovery.pdf.

5   Mihm, Christopher J., *Partnering for resilience: A practical approach to emergency preparedness*, IBM Institute for Business Value: Research Brief, in collaboration with IBM Center for The Business of Government, and the National Academy of Public Administration (NAPA), 2022, https://www.businessofgovernment.org/sites/default/files/Partnering%20for%20Resilience.pdf.

6   Grand Challenges in Public Administration: An Agenda for the Future of Governance, National Academy of Public Administration, Washington D.C., 2021, https://s3.us-west-2.amazonaws.com/napa-2021/Grand-Challenges-Booklet-FINAL.pdf.

7   Hefferan, p.xii.

PART I | ROADMAPS TO GOVERNMENT RESILIENCY

Chapter One

Emergency Preparedness and Response

INTRODUCTION

After an unprecedented number of catastrophic events over the past three years, the field of emergency management has been thrust into the spotlight. From the continuing global COVID-19 pandemic and debilitating cyberattacks to weather extremes such as deadly heat waves, "100-year floods," raging wildfires, and more, together these shocks have stressed governments, businesses, communities, and individuals while raising fundamental questions about what is needed to prepare for and respond to future crises.

This chapter focuses on the complex and cross-cutting nature of disasters that do not respect geography, jurisdiction, political, or organizational boundaries. Emergency management should follow suit, recognizing that the key to success is the strength of the network before, during, and after a disaster. This chapter reflects on what governments can do in the near term to better prepare and respond to emergent situations. Recommendations and a host of associated action steps conclude this chapter.

Setting the Context

Disasters are complex and crosscutting by nature. They have no respect for geographic, jurisdictional, political, or organizational boundaries. Emergency management should follow suit. Preparedness and response cannot be the sole responsibility of one sector, one program, one agency, or one level of government. Rather, the key to success—and the root cause of many failures when absent—is the strength of the network before, during, and after a disaster through partnerships established between sectors, levels of government, and agencies. Simply put, radical horizontal and vertical problems cannot be solved in silos.

The pandemic highlighted serious weaknesses in the global supply chain, hampering government responses to life-threatening situations. When governments do respond by creating assistance programs to offset financial hardship resulting from economic impacts, these programs can increase exposure to fraud, waste, and abuse.

COVID-19 revealed the evolving and complex risks that government agencies confront. Yet as the pandemic recedes, this risk landscape will remain. Many risks—aging IT systems, cybersecurity threats, supply chain

Source: The IBM Center report, Partnering for Resilience: A Practical Approach to Emergency Preparedness, *by Chris Mihm, Syracuse University—as well as informed by the Future Shock Roundtable discussion and resources.*

vulnerabilities, impacts of climate shifts, workforce skills gaps, or program integrity—have the potential to disrupt government programs, mission support operations, and the ability of governments to conduct the business of government. Government resilience follows from the resilience of its institutions.[1]

Critical Components for Emergency Preparedness and Response

Emergency management is complex and nuanced, with contributions from a diverse set of stakeholders including the public, business community, civil society, and all levels of government. A vast body of research and literature informs the topic of emergency management. Below are some critical components of emergency preparedness and response and building resilience going forward.

- **Risk management and capability assessment.** Governments and agencies need an evolving understanding of potential risks and vulnerabilities, and how they may change over time. Understanding potential impact can inform a risk mitigation strategy. In addition, governments must be able to measure current capabilities at all levels—federal, state, provincial, local, tribal, etc.—to identify gaps and set realistic capability targets.

- **Precrisis planning, communication, and coordination.** The confusion and disorientation following the onset of a shock requires that much coordination is needed ahead of time to identify roles and responsibilities during an emergency response exercise. Coordinating at the interagency level as well as across borders poses challenges but is critical to successful response.

- **Testing.** Effective testing that provides accurate assessment of response capabilities, including first responder health and well-being, is needed. Insights gained from testing must result in plans-of-action to address and retest areas of deficiency.

- **Situational awareness and communication.** Real-time, quality information is difficult to obtain in times of crisis. Yet the quality of information matters greatly for quality decision making and effective response. Misinformation and disinformation further complicate the ability of decision makers and those at risk during a crisis to make sound judgments and take decisive action.

- **Transparency and trust.** The public must have trust in government agencies providing emergency response services. A large component of that trust involves sharing accurate information with the public at appropriate times. Distrust and a lack of trust can blunt the effectiveness of emergency responses, and disrupt coordination between responders and the public. Also, emergency response must also plan for and account for serving the most vulnerable of the population, whose safety can require unique capabilities and whose ability to move away from danger can be limited.

- **Learning and accountability.** Government agencies need to systematically gather and apply lessons learned. They must further be accountable to their citizens for maintaining public order and offering emergency responses.

Insights and Recommendations

What specific and practical steps can governments take in the near term to better prepare and respond? Insights from the Future Shocks initiative were provided by leaders from the U.S. Federal Emergency Management Agency (FEMA), the Organization for Economic Cooperation and Development (OECD), the International Association of Emergency Managers, the former Governor of Maryland and former Commandant of the Coast Guard, and a cross-section of experts from key stakeholder groups.

The following recommendations emerged from discussion with these leaders and associated research. These steps do not constitute an exhaustive list of actions, but rather reflect suggestions made by these experts.

Strengthen the emergency preparedness and response network

As the adage goes, the middle of a crisis is not the time to be exchanging business cards. Networks with clearly defined roles, responsibilities, leadership, and accountability must be built well before an event takes place.

FEMA offers one example of a network philosophy for emergency response. The agency strives to adopt a whole community approach that "attempts to engage the full capacity of the private and nonprofit sectors—including businesses, faith-based and disability organizations, and the American public—in conjunction with the participation of state, local, tribal, territorial, and federal governmental partners."[2]

This complex approach can be difficult to execute. The nature of the U.S. intergovernmental system can create tension between the federal government and the states. Relationships can also be strained among states and their cities and localities. While structural issues are unlikely to ever be fully resolved, leaders need to untangle differing authorities, priorities, and demands to limit misunderstandings and confusion during a crisis. Using Memoranda of Agreement (MOAs), continuous training, and tabletop exercises, agencies can define and reinforce roles, responsibilities, and working relationships across levels of government. Ultimately, successful emergency response networks result from preexisting organizational and—at least as important—personal relationships. In building the network, planners should also recognize that private and nonprofit involvement is not just helpful or additive—it can determine the success of the response.

These organizations collectively bring resources, community relationships, capacities, and agility that governments lack. They need to be involved as central partners in preparedness planning.

Strengthening the emergency preparedness and response network requires a cultural change for many organizations. Working across sectors with differing values, attitudes, operating models, and accountability mechanisms is not easy. Organizations are typically more comfortable operating within existing programmatic boundaries than working within a broader network, as one participant among many and not directing efforts or being in full control. As an example, FEMA and the U.S. Department of Housing and Urban Development could transfer responsibilities more smoothly as emergency response transitions into the longer-term recovery phase. Recognizing and pursuing the value that can be delivered through partnerships is critical to the strength of the network.

ACTION STEPS

- Clearly define the roles and responsibilities of organizations within the emergency response network.

- Tap into private and nonprofit resources as part of preparedness planning.

- Evaluate organizational culture for openness to working with partners.

Build local capacity

Local governments and agencies sit on the frontline of most crises, facing unique threats, economic and social contexts, and capacities to respond.

Local governments can position themselves to respond better in several specific ways, including conducting risk-based, all-hazard preparedness planning, working with the private sector, and accessing and managing intergovernmental assistance—especially when receiving recovery funds, the point when local governments assume even greater responsibility in the aftermath of a disaster.

Jointly coordinated capacity development among localities, mutual aid agreements, regional compacts, and financial incentives for localities to build their capacity can also facilitate the abilities of local governments to respond. Additionally, they can use online learning environments to share experiences and identify and exchange successful practices. Finally, as Baby Boomers continue to exit the workforce, local governments can recruit and retain the public-spirited Millennial and Gen Z generations.

ACTION STEPS

- Build partnerships with the private sector to expand response capacity.

- Extend reach with regional partnerships.

- Evaluate emergency management plans to determine if they apply to a wide range of disasters.

Put community engagement and meeting diverse needs at the center of preparedness efforts

With distrust the default emotion in nearly 60 percent of people surveyed by Edelman in their annual trust barometer, building trust with constituents becomes even more critical to effective emergency response.[3]

This begins with recognizing that different parts of a community have vastly dissimilar needs and capabilities during an emergency. For example, physical or financial barriers, pressing medical needs, disabilities, and fears of relocating are among the reasons people may not evacuate from harm's way. An emergency preparedness and response network must address the diverse needs and abilities of all segments of a community well before a disaster occurs, and tailor planning and response efforts accordingly.

Emergency planners can leverage robust and inclusive public participation programs to create informed planning and response strategies that reflect the needs of the local community. These programs also help to ensure public understanding and acceptance of the resulting decisions.

Communication strategies must also be adapted to reach the different populations, considering what information is communicated, how it is communicated, and by whom. This entails identifying and working closely with trusted voices in the community to establish confidence and understanding. As seen with the COVID-19 pandemic response and evacuation orders for impending weather disasters, it can be difficult to convince some individuals to act, even given clear and imminent danger. Trusted voices from the community can help overcome this challenge.

ACTION STEPS

- Establish programs to involve the public in response planning.

- Identify the factors that affect the ability of people within a community—particularly hard-to-reach communities—to react to significant events.

- Identify the voices that constituents trust and ways to partner with them to share key messages.

Dedicate sufficient and flexible resources

The most devastating aspect of disasters involves harm inflicted on people and communities, including injuries and loss of life. But disaster response and recovery are also exceedingly expensive.

Since 1980 for the U.S. alone, the cumulative costs of disasters, where damages reached or exceeded $1 billion in cost, is well over $2 trillion.[4] However, as an expert who contributed insights to the Future Shocks initiative astutely observed, "If you think responding to a disaster is costly, try doing that without upfront preparation." While certainly correct, most governments face competing priorities for funding, with insufficient attention given to events considered rare and not entirely predictable—even though it appears they are growing more frequent and more catastrophic.

As the nature and prevalence of emergencies increase—especially those related to climate change—the operational and response burden on agencies at each level of government has grown significantly as well. Simultaneous disasters strain budgets and stress organizations and staff. For the short-term, two actions are recommended:

- First, establish flexibility in funding streams within each level of government and across levels of government, so that funds can move quickly across organizations to respond to a crisis. Political leaders have an understandable desire for spending transparency and accountability. The puzzle is how to achieve those important values while also rapidly and seamlessly assisting people in need, and minimizing administrative burdens resulting from funding silos and assistance requirements.

- Second, explore ways to align a greater understanding of risks to budget processes. The Biden administration has acted in this regard with a directive to quantify climate-change-driven risks to the federal budget.[5] This initiative could be expanded to different levels of government.

ACTION STEPS

- Identify and remove the barriers that are blocking smooth transfers of funds among response organizations within the network.

- Initiate risk quantification within budget processes.

- Identify ways technology can facilitate more cost-effective emergency responses.

Establish a data strategy well before disaster strikes

Decision makers across governments, businesses, and the public require high quality and credible data to guide organizational and personal decisions.

In fact, data feeds the effective communication techniques discussed earlier. Both clarity of message based on evidence and rapid response to disinformation are essential in crisis communications. Unfortunately, the complex nature of most emergencies and the plethora of communications channels typically result in multiple "sources of truth," leading to confusion, a lack of trust, and disjointed decision making.

Emergency preparedness and response networks should agree on key data elements well before an emergency occurs. For example, they can define data elements consistently across the network, agree on data needed in real time and how it will be collected, and identify how to make data available to those who need it in formats they can readily use. The network's data strategy also should include an assessment of the technology needed to gather and report data in real time as well as initiatives to fill any technology gaps, such as distributed analytics built on hybrid cloud networks and the use of artificial intelligence to rationalize large data stores rapidly.

ACTION STEPS

- Tap into data analytics to fuel more efficient crisis management and more effective crisis communications.

- Identify and implement a technology infrastructure that supports data sharing across a network of emergency responders.

- Implement data management programs that facilitate high-quality data for sharing while aligning with data privacy requirements.

Establish workforce strategies to meet current, surge, and future needs
U.S., state, and local governments lost more than 600,000 workers between the start of the pandemic and June 2022, affecting their ability to maintain basic services as well as respond to critical situations.[6]

Challenges in acquiring and retaining mission-critical skills can be particularly acute for agencies involved in emergency preparedness and response. The diversity of the skill sets required, the need for surge capacity during emergencies, and the evolving missions of organizations to accommodate the overlapping nature of emergencies create additional staffing problems for preparedness and response across all levels of government.

Important work on how to tackle the talent deficit can offer some direction. For example, the National Academy of Public Administration's "No Time to Wait" reports provide a roadmap focused on changing the human capital culture from one of compliance to a "promise of performance."[7] The report recommended the establishment of a competency-based talent management model that:

- Identifies the core competencies of occupational and professional groups

- Trains employees in the competencies they will need, and certifies them (with credentials or "badges") for the skills they bring

- Creates flexible teams that match the competencies needed with the teams' missions

- Establishes communities of practice among occupations and professional groups to foster continuous learning about the skills employees need

- Devises a plan for reskilling the government's workforce to match mission requirements with employees' skills

- Helps ensure that employees' skills keep up with hyper-fast changes in mission

Agencies do not just need more people with specific skills. For community engagement and equity to reside at the center of response efforts, governments need to make sure their employees reflect the diversity of the communities they serve. A diverse and inclusive staff recruitment, hiring, and development program is vital to achieving this.

The overwhelming stress faced by frontline workers and first responders—who in many cases are themselves survivors of the disaster—underscores the importance of attention to burnout as well as the physical and mental health and well-being of staff. Numerous reports from hospital nurses and other frontline medical workers during COVID-19 vividly illustrated the enormous emotional toll from being at the center of a long-term emergency response.[8] While awareness is important, action to address the welfare of employees is an imperative. This could include developing rapid assistance networks for the well-being of first responders, as well as discussions to develop an understanding of accessible mental health services.

ACTION STEPS

- Identify opportunities to streamline or automate processes using technology.

- Establish training programs to retrain and reskill current workers, aligning skills with mission requirements.

- Work with experts to cultivate a culture focused on employee well-being.

LOOKING FORWARD

As evidenced by the past few years, response to crisis events requires collaboration—within communities, and across federal, state, local, and country jurisdictions. From building the response and community networks, to defining communication and data sharing strategies, to addressing budget and workforce challenges, these approaches offer a starting point—a valuable set of practical and actionable ideas that governments can employ to better support their citizens and employees confronting more frequent and more destructive disasters.

In the end dedicating time and resources can create mechanisms and capacity with the goal of being better prepared for future disruptive events. As observed in the IBM Center report, *Managing the Next Crisis: Twelve Principles for Dealing with Viral Uncertainty*, governments confront a cascade of "unknown unknowns" (the category of unknowable events that tend to be the difficult ones), for which anticipatory measures can take years or decades to develop.[9]

Indeed, the nation will likely face far more uncertainty in the future, making effective responses more important. This new operating reality affords government leaders an opportunity to reflect, learn, and build organizations that are more agile, adaptive, innovative, and able to mobilize swiftly and operate in new ways. Now more than ever, government leaders can take a holistic view of the managing of risk and building resiliency, prioritizing what they do know and preparing for what they don't.

Endnotes

1   Chenok, Daniel J., G. Edward DeSeve, Margie Graves, Michael J. Keegan, Mark Newsome, Karin O'Leary. *Eight Strategies for Transforming Government.* IBM Center for The Business of Government, Washington D.C., 2022, p.32, https://bit.ly/3rcAYUt.

2   "A Whole Community Approach to Emergency Management: Principles, Themes, and Pathways for Action." FEMA. FDOC 104-008-1. December 2011, https://www.fema.gov/sites/default/files/2020-07/whole_community_dec2011__2.pdf.

3   "The Trust 10." Edelman Trust Barometer 2022, https://www.edelman.com/sites/g/files/aatuss191/files/2022-01/Trust%2022_Top10.pdf.

4   NOAA National Centers for Environmental Information (NCEI) U.S. Billion-Dollar Weather and Climate Disasters (2023), https://www.ncei.noaa.gov/access/billions/. DOI:10.25921/stkw-7w73.

5   Fact Sheet: President Biden Directs Agencies to Analyze and Mitigate the Risk Climate Change Poses to Homeowners and Consumers, Businesses and Workers, and the Financial System and Federal Government Itself." White House statement. May 20, 2021, https://bit.ly/46rGF0v.

6   Brey, Jared. "Government Worker Shortages Worsen Crisis Response." *Governing: The Future of States and Localities.* October 3, 2022, https://www.governing.com/work/government-worker-shortages-worsen-crisis-response.

7   National Academy of Public Administration. "No Time to Wait: Building a Public Service for the 21st Century." July 2017; "No Time to Wait, Part 2: Building a Public Service for the 21st Century." September 2018, https://napawash.org/academy-studies/no-time-to-wait-part-2-building-a-public-service-for-the-21st-century.

8   Murthy, Dr. Vivek H. "Perspective: Confronting Health Worker Burnout and Well-Being." *New England Journal of Medicine.* 387:577-579. August 18, 2022, https://www.nejm.org/doi/full/10.1056/NEJMp2207252.

9   Barrett, Katherine, Richard Greene, and Donald F Kettl. *Managing the Next Crisis: Twelve Principles for Dealing with Viral Uncertainty.* IBM Center for The Business of Government, https://www.businessofgovernment.org/sites/default/files/Managing%20the%20Next%20Crisis_0.pdf.

Chapter Two

Cybersecurity

INTRODUCTION

Since the advent of the internet, criminal groups, hacktivists, and state-sponsored threat actors have put governments in the crosshairs of cyber-crime. During the last half of 2022, the number of cyberattacks targeting governments increased by 95 percent worldwide, compared to the same period in 2021.[1] The cost of public sector data breaches also increased 7.25 percent between March 2021 and March 2022, with an average cost per incident of $2.07 million.[2]

Government digital platforms—and the sensitive information they store—represent target-rich environments. Economic globalization and digital interconnection of nearly every aspect of commercial and government activity have created an intricate digital ecosystem. Cyberspace has reshaped physical borders and governance models, and global networks mean that the impacts of threats and incidents can quickly escalate in magnitude and breadth if not addressed with speed and effectiveness.

This chapter examines today's complex cyber threat environment, and the government's responsibility to secure a safe and secure digital ecosystem. It focuses how best to reduce the impact of cyber incidents by developing and implementing cybersecurity strategies that promote resilience through public-private partnerships. The chapter recommends a series of actions designed to help governments emerge stronger from current and future cyber shocks.

Setting the Context

The adverse use of cyber tools by nation states and by other actors threatens national security, disrupts government service delivery and our daily existence, and supports criminal activity. And artificial intelligence (AI) can defend against nefarious activity, and also be an enabler. Research on areas where progress can be made is essential. Some of these areas were outlined in the Presidential Executive Order 14028 on Improving the Nation's Cybersecurity, and include:

- Improvements in threat information sharing between the government and private sector

Source: The IBM Center report, Preparing Governments for Future Shocks: An Action Plan to Build Cyber Resilience in a World of Uncertainty, *by Tony Scott, CEO of Intrusion, Inc.—as well as informed by the Future Shock Roundtable discussion and resources.*

- Government use of stronger cybersecurity standards such as zero trust architectures, encryption, and multifactor authentication

- Improvements in software supply chain assurance

- Improvements in detection, response to, and recovery from cyber incidents

One recent cyber incident illustrated gaps in security in government, commercial enterprises, and critical infrastructure. The Solar Winds incident showed vulnerabilities in the software development lifecycle process and the global supply chain. In the area of software supply chain assurance, "DevSecOps" principles can drive ecosystems for developing software based on those principles. As highlighted in a recent IBM Center report, *Achieving Mission Outcomes Through DevSecOps* by Margie Graves, using DevSecOps supports a preapproved software development environment where developers can experiment. Developers can code, test, prove, or disprove initial hypotheses about how the code will work, adjust the software build according to what they learn, and then continue iterating. Capability and features are developed into viable products. Security is incorporated into the build, and continuously tested.

Another recent incident, the ransomware attack on Colonial Pipeline, illustrated another vulnerability. The White House has initiated international partnerships to accelerate cooperation on improving network resilience, addressing the financial systems that make ransomware profitable, disrupting the ransomware ecosystem via law enforcement collaboration, and leveraging the tools of diplomacy to address safe harbors and improve partner capacity. AI has emerged as a key tool to guard against such attacks. Key questions that leaders addressed in considering cybersecurity resiliency as part of the Future Shocks initiative are summarized on the following two pages.

Key Questions for Protecting Cybersecurity and Critical Infrastructure

Fostering resilience and continuity of operations. Threats to undermine both organizational resilience and continuity of operations include shocks such as ransomware and climate catastrophe.

 How can governments define a base level of preparedness required to withstand shocks and continue to provide essential citizen services?

Adapting governance to a shared responsibility model. Governments must plan for and evaluate cybersecurity governance in terms of defining responsibility for defense and resilience and develop policies and standards that align to agency missions (including modernizing security governance to support the implementation of zero trust principles).

 How can partners best work across the broader ecosystem in addressing potential threats and the societal impact of cyberattacks?

Coordinating with stakeholders across all levels of government. Threats exist at all levels of government—national, state, local, tribal, and territorial. Some actions to take involve combining resources, activating public-private partnerships, coordinating incident response, and sharing leading practices.

 How can communication informed by cyber expertise help governments understand policy gaps, implement coordinated policy solutions, and still maintain privacy?

Modernizing security of critical infrastructure. Defending critical infrastructure requires both an understanding of systems and a defense strategy that repels attacks but also has robust intrusion response.

 How can governments work with industry to help make security intrinsic to infrastructure architecture and system design and more frictionless for end users?

Standardizing cyber incident response. An incident response strategy must be established well before a cyber incident. This should include robust testing and training processes and an efficient communications framework.

 How can governments identify and engage stakeholders across domains?

Key Questions for Enabling Hybrid and Distributed Work

Using automation and connectivity to optimize capacity, skills, and resources. Building new capabilities around connected devices and connected services, embracing modernization and emerging technologies, and developing new technologies that keep pace with advancing threats.

 How can governments work with industry and academia to stay ahead of the innovation curve and develop resilient systems, given potential threats to cyber, physical, and natural hazards?

Improving security hygiene. Understanding the collective impact of human behavior. Developing strong cyber hygiene for all individuals acting in both private and professional capacities is essential.

 What strategies can all stakeholders take to promote security ABCs— awareness, behaviors, and culture?

Developing the cyber workforce. Anticipating skill demand, identifying talent gaps, and attracting and retaining talent in key security positions represent issues that government and industry are dealing with in many domains—issues addressed in a recent congressionally-mandated NAPA report for DHS CISA.[3]

 How can we meet current and future cybersecurity demand, via better engagement with traditional and nontraditional sources of talent?

Re-envisioning technology, security, and data integrity as public goods. Security concerns exist for many forms of technology that are based on implicit trust, including the dissemination of misinformation and disinformation through social media. Additionally, many platforms operate across multiple levels of government and across international borders, introducing complex operational and compliance demands.

 How can leaders reinforce the public's ability to securely access networks with accurate, high-value information anytime, anyplace, anywhere?

Recognizing the significance of emerging technologies, including quantum computing. Anticipating new threats from technology innovations, including the dangers posed to existing digital encryption protocols by quantum exploits as well as new ways of working with solutions based on distributed (versus centralized) authority (e.g., consensus-based solutions, distributed ledgers).

 How should governments prepare for the future by addressing security vulnerabilities created by new technologies such as quantum computing and blockchain?

Insights and Recommendations

In recognition of today's complex cyber threat environment, and the government's responsibility to secure a safe and secure digital ecosystem, the White House announced a comprehensive National Cybersecurity Strategy in March 2023. This strategy sets a path to make cyber defense easier and more cost-effective. It also focuses on reducing the impact of cyber incidents through resiliency and aligning efforts with national values to secure the promise of a digital future.

U.S. and global leaders participating the Future Shocks Cybersecurity Roundtable outlined a series of recommendations designed to help governments emerge stronger from current and future cyber shocks.

Increase the cyber talent resource base

To address the rapidly growing gap between supply and demand for cybersecurity professionals, governments can work to increase the cyber talent resource base as an action at the top of the list of actionable priorities. Cyber skill shortfalls impact a broad set of disciplines including analysis and engineering, software development, threat intelligence, penetration testing, auditing and consulting, digital forensics, and cryptography. Moreover, because many private sector employers offer higher compensation for cybersecurity positions, governments are often at a disadvantage when recruiting for analysts, responders, security architects, developers, managers, and other roles also in demand by private sector employers.

While massive digitization remakes economic sectors, digital technology is also transforming how services are designed and delivered. Consequently, cyber disruptions are becoming more common and further reaching, putting even more pressure on government-based cybersecurity resources.

Options for Developing the Cyber Talent Pipeline

Options to develop the cyber talent pipeline feeding government include:

- Waive the requirement of a four-year college degree for some skilled areas.

- Include cyber education early in K-12 curricula.

- Tighten the focus on reskilling people already in the workforce.

- Develop multidisciplinary programs, such as cyber plus business and cyber plus medical.

- Expand cybersecurity apprenticeship programs.

- Increase the number of women in STEM educational programs—and cyber education in particular—by making these fields more attractive for women.

- Reinforce workforce actions at the state and local level and in the business community, where decisions can impact workforce outcomes.

- Leverage the supply of military veterans with cyber skills and develop more veteran training programs that focus on cyber skills.

- Reexamine selected high barriers to entry into cyber careers, such as mandatory security clearances and required baseline skill sets.

- Strengthen the cybersecurity workforce by promoting diversity, equity, inclusion, and accessibility.

In addition to these observations, the National Academy of Public Administration recently released a report about the government's role in building a cybersecurity workforce. This call to action can be accessed here: https://napawash.org/academy-studies/dhs-cybersecurity-workforce.

ACTION STEPS

- Ensuring that governmental organizations can meet the cybersecurity staffing challenge will require a multipronged effort and new thinking to recruit talent from a wider population.

Improve organizational collaboration for faster response

Collaboration and information sharing between national and international governmental organizations—as well as between government and business stakeholders—are complex and slow moving.

Despite recent progress in improving public-private coordination,[4] increased cooperation between cyberattackers continues to be an ongoing threat. Threat actors are developing and promoting criminal infrastructures and services that hostile governments and gangs can use for illegitimate purposes.

Bad actors are also adopting new technologies quickly to penetrate networks and thwart efforts to contain threats, which can be difficult to counter when those efforts depend on coordination across entities with differing standards, missions, and priorities.

Coordination and collaboration are key themes in the National Cybersecurity Strategy paper released by the White House in March 2023. This strategy stresses partnerships between civil society and industry, and boosts collaboration with allies to strengthen norms of responsible state behavior, hold countries accountable for irresponsible behavior, and disrupt criminal networks behind cyberattacks.

A lack of transparency exists in the many interdependencies, complexities, and related risks of digitally connected services. As a result, the public often has difficulty understanding the fragility of systems and the cascading effects associated with service disruption, including the impacts on downstream suppliers and partners.

Examples of such interdependencies include open-source software, supply chains, and critical infrastructures that increasingly rely on technology services for operations, fulfillment, and platform security. Emerging ecosystems concentrated on coordinated economic activities need to be more aware of their shared responsibility for cybersecurity and resilience.

Methods to improve collaboration include:

- Focus on broad, policy-driven cybersecurity initiatives to establish baselines for critical infrastructure and close gaps in regulatory frameworks.

- Strengthen law enforcement capabilities.

- Prioritize standard cyber risk assessment frameworks to facilitate more efficient collaboration.

- Accelerate feedback loops and improve sensor capabilities to correct for over- and under-estimates of cyber risk.

- Conduct cyber incident response training to coordinate operational support across ecosystem partners and use drill exercises to improve resiliency across public and private sectors.

- Share cyber expertise and costs across agencies involved with digital operations and service provision, and support agencies not equipped to provide for their own security from common government or commercial centers of cyber excellence.

- Take advantage of shared cyber services more broadly, and secure cloud services in particular, along the lines of the U.S. Department of Homeland Security Cyber Safety Review Board.[5]

- Encourage proactive investment to prepare for threats coming from advances in AI and quantum computing technologies.

- Use AI and automation technologies to strengthen cyber defenses more broadly and counter the use of these technologies by cyber adversaries and threat actors.

ACTION STEPS

- In response to threat actors quickly adapting new technologies to penetrate networks and thwart countermeasures, governments must increase collaboration and expedite information sharing to stay a step ahead.

Align public and private sector cybersecurity priorities

By identifying common challenges, sharing best practices, and exploring avenues for cooperation, numerous areas exist for industry and government cooperation to improve cybersecurity on a broad scale. High-priority opportunities for alignment include:

- Emphasize recruiting from a wider array of backgrounds for the cyber workforce.

- Sharpen focus on security innovation as a competitive advantage.

- Support zero-trust frameworks that assume network security is always at risk to internal and external threats.

- Institutionalize continuous and pervasive cyber education from "K through Gray."

- Improve understanding of cyber issues among elected officials and their support staff, as well as key government decision makers.

- Improve cybersecurity expectations, standards, metrics, and data to strengthen understanding of threats, and the need for public and private investment to counteract and contain the threats.

ACTION STEPS

- Ensure that governments and businesses are addressing key cybersecurity priorities and consistently implementing best practices for mutual benefit.

Study ways to bolster democratic institutions against cyberattacks

Cyber warfare actors target the functions of democratic states and institutions through misinformation and disinformation campaigns. These attacks are designed to influence public support and involvement in electoral, legislative, or regulatory processes, and include attempts to steer public opinion or undermine democratic norms of behavior.

While the primary objective of these overt or covert campaigns is to sow confusion and promote social discord in the near term, longer-term efforts could succeed in swaying public opinion. Due to the complexities represented by these cyber challenges to representative forms of government, a broad consensus has yet to be formed on the most effective ways to defend against this growing threat—more research into measures that can counter cyber threats to democracy is needed.

Additional challenges include:

- State-backed efforts to shape public opinion through the broad suppression of public information available on media platforms. For example, China, Russia, and other authoritarian regimes engage in search engine restrictions and strict censorship policies.

- Consumer behavior information collected by popular mobile social media applications, such as TikTok.

- The potential for highly automated and effective disinformation campaigns in more open democracies presents asymmetric threats that are difficult to identify and counter. This topic requires more in-depth research to understand the implications in terms of cyber risk, threats, and resiliency.

ACTION STEPS

- Misinformation and disinformation campaigns have the potential to sway public opinion and undermine democracy, and more research is needed on methods to defend against these threats.

LOOKING FORWARD

Just as prior waves of dramatic technological innovation have impacted our society and our common welfare, today's massive digitization has wide-ranging implications.

Global reliance on open technology underscores what makes communities prosper—notably social connectivity, communications, and collaboration. These factors drive national and international well-being; at the same time, reliance on digital interactions makes them prime targets for cybercriminals.

Current safeguards work some of the time but fall short in too many cases. Government leaders need to adopt more proactive measures to get ahead of risks. While technology shapes the consumption of information and the platforms used for social discourse, the growing sophistication of cyber threats impacts public and private sector stakeholders around the world.

Governments have a vital role in working with key stakeholders to identify cyber risks. This starts with building response capacity and resilience in the face of these risks. But government officials need to go further—executing leadership agendas that drive change toward a more resilient future, while also reflecting the unique identity and sense of purpose that defines each government in the eyes of their constituents.

Taken together, the insights and recommendations outlined in this chapter provide a viable road map for governments to follow in the continual improvement of their cybersecurity posture. Government agencies, reliance on digital networks in the response and recovery from the pandemic will likely only grow in their efforts to weather an uncertain future.

Endnotes

1   Venkat, Apurva. "Cyberattacks against governments jumped 95% in last half of 2022, CloudSek says." CSO. January 4, 2023, https://www.csoonline.com/article/574275/cyberattacks-against-governments-jumped-95-in-last-half-of-2022-cloudsek-says.html.

2   "Cost of a Data Breach Report 2022." IBM Security. July 2022, https://www.ibm.com/downloads/cas/3R8N1DZJ.

3   A Call to Action: The Federal Government's Role in Building a Cybersecurity Workforce for the Future, https://napawash.org/academy-studies/dhs-cybersecurity-workforce.

4   Readout of Cybersecurity Executive Forum on Electric Vehicles and Electric Vehicle Charging Infrastructure Hosted by the Office of the National Cyber Director. The White House Briefing Room. October 25, 2022.

5   "DHS Launches First-Ever Cyber Safety Review Board." U.S. Department of Homeland Security. February 3, 2022, https://www.dhs.gov/news/2022/02/03/dhs-launches-first-ever-cyber-safety-review-board.

Chapter Three

Supply Chain

INTRODUCTION

During the last three years, a perfect storm of natural and geopolitical events has disrupted worldwide supply chains in ways that few governments could have anticipated. Even as nations, businesses, and consumers strive to normalize, new interruptions have created bottlenecks in an enormously complicated and interconnected system of purchasing, operation, distribution, integration, and consumption.

This chapter explores the role governments play in preparing for supply chain disruptions. It assesses how governments can foresee potential challenges, plan responses ahead of time, and be ready to minimize the impacts of supply chain disruptions. It outlines insights and recommendations on how best to diagnose threats, design responses, sustain supply chains, and mitigate disruptions by building supply chain immunity.

Setting the Context

In a 2022 survey, 38 percent of global CEOs reported that supply chain disruption is one of their greatest challenges.[1] And now, the impact of supply chain disruptions on national economies and social systems is driving government leaders to also put a top priority on building supply chain resiliency.

In the U.S., disaster and emergency events have typically been regional and limited in duration; examples include hurricanes, floods, fires, earthquakes, industrial accidents, or terrorist attacks. In all such cases, events generally evoked immediate action from emergency responders. The response to large scale disasters typically involves distribution of critical medical and disaster response supplies to surrounding regions, often following an established procedure for procuring and distributing supplies (e.g., food, shelter, water, and relief goods). Supplies are normally readily available, and past disaster response efforts have involved few problems in identifying qualified local suppliers for immediate contracting, acquisition, and shipping to impacted sites.

The COVID-19 pandemic was dramatically different. The national response infrastructure has never encountered an emergency where every industry sector was affected by disruptions at the same time. Government agencies were unfamiliar with how to address a disaster of this magnitude, which impacted every state in the country, every industry, every population, every hospital. The pandemic revealed significant gaps in the government's response capacity to this crisis, and response efforts have been the subject of many task forces and inquiries.

Source: The IBM Center report, Preparing Governments for Future Shocks: Collaborating to Build Resilient Supply Chains *by Professor Robert Handfield, North Carolina State University—as well as informed by the Future Shock Roundtable discussion and resources.*

The president's FY2023 budget request to Congress focused significant attention and investment proposals on strengthening supply chain operations and improving supply chain risk management and resiliency. The execution of these programs can be transformed by leveraging a "whole of government" scope and industry-leading supply chain management and shared services business models to their delivery. The box below highlights leading supply chain practices.

Current Leading Practices in
Supply Chain Resilience and Preparedness

Digital transformation across interconnected processes and extended ecosystems with the expansion of new automation technologies provides predictability, flexibility, and intelligence to operations—especially in the automating of decision making. AI and intelligent, automated workflows can deliver 360-degree insights and impact analysis that provide this interconnectivity and optimize predictability. These workflows can benefit the workforce—digital and human—to dynamically adjust to the unforeseen with both self-learning and self-calibration.

With digital transformation comes increased vulnerabilities and security concerns for supply chains, including critical infrastructure, which is essential for supply chain performance. Additionally, there is an escalating need for visibility into who are comprising supply chain networks as well as transparency, providing that knowledge to external stakeholders. Leveraging digital transformation and intelligent workflows can address security concerns and make this visibility possible.

Current leading practices

As organizations implement technology into their supply chain practices, the following actions can help in their digital transformation:

- Use AI and machine learning to guide the quality and track performance of workflow reactions and decisions, as well as to monitor physical assets with predictability.

- Digitize to develop agile workflows to react quickly to escalating situations.

- Begin experimenting with quantum computing tools and methods to lay the groundwork for expanded capabilities.

- Combine predictive and prescriptive analysis for better decision making, while focusing on micro-insights revealed through extreme digitalization.

Current Leading Practices in
Supply Chain Diversification

By its very definition, a chain is a series of entities linked, connected, or associated together. Extending that concept, a modern supply chain connects the organizations, activities, people, information, and resources that intersect to move products and services from producers to suppliers to end consumption—and now, with a focus on circularity, back again. These ecosystems are complex, interconnected, and global. They are ecosystems of partners, infrastructure, and resources.

Many organizations are investing in regionalization and localization strategies of product supply and production to decrease the risk of overreliance on a single region. Many are parsing the supply chain by segment to promote tighter collaboration with suppliers and service providers that have differentiated skills and capabilities—adding AI and algorithmic insights for increased risk management and predictive event forecasting.

Current Leading Practices

To be successful, modern supply chains operate through an ecosystem of partners and actions, outlined below, that can enable an organization to diversify their supply chain models:

- Use segmentation techniques to examine ecosystems in minute detail for increased collaborative opportunities across workflows with data-infused intelligent decision and action.

- Increase visibility and security in every touchpoint of supply chain workflows with extended ecosystems and partners.

- Reevaluate supplier networks with n-tier visibility and trusted data-sharing.

Current Leading Practices in
Supply Chain Operations and Sustainability

An emerging perspective among forward-thinking leaders is that open innovation with business partners drives sustainability initiatives and transformation. In fact, many are finding a stronger alignment between their sustainability strategies and digital transformation initiatives.

Leaders from both public and private sectors are focused on improving energy efficiency, water management, and using more organic and recyclable materials—reporting that these sustainability initiatives will substantially change their supply chain models over the next two to three years.

Workflow digitization also contributes to helping organizations meet their sustainability objectives. As teams evaluate and build intelligent workflows, they can incorporate ways to reduce their environmental impact and move toward comprehensive circularity programs. In these programs, end-of-life products are not disposed of, they flow back into the supply chain.

Current Leading Practices

Sustainability initiatives are growing in importance within all facets of an organization's operations—including its supply chain model. The following actions can help with the integration of sustainability and supply chain operations:

- Optimize workflows with AI, automation, and virtualization to manage carbon, waste, energy, and water consumption.

- Use virtualization to help shrink environmental footprints and support the nine R's of circularity: Recycle, Reduce, Reuse, Repair, Refurbish, Remanufacture, Repurpose, Recover, Refuse.

- Experiment with open innovation and scientific discovery to explore future solutions and possibilities.

Insights and Recommendations

What is the role of governments in preparing for supply chain disruptions that impact government services, national defense, and national economies? How can governments foresee potential challenges, plan responses ahead of time, and be ready to minimize the impacts?

Insights from the Future Shocks roundtables and related research suggest that governments can establish a shared service center of excellence to develop protection against supply chain disruptions. After establishing these supply chain risk management organizations, governments should have the centralized resources to diagnose threats, design responses, sustain supply chains, and mitigate disruptions by building supply chain immunity.[2]

Create a shared service approach to build supply chain resiliency
Many disruptive scenarios require different responses from multiple government entities. This leads to a clear conclusion: to garner multiagency support and cross-sector collaboration for quick response, a shared service strategy can be a key form of engagement to build supply chain resiliency.

A shared service approach for supply chains would also incorporate a "center of excellence" (COE) model. A COE would consist of multiple agencies, and could include a data center with key information, predictive modeling capabilities, and an effective vendor-managed inventory. A multiagency shared service, with full-time subject matter experts contributing unique expertise and perspectives on supply chain disruption events. This team could also build out diagnostic data and organize more predictive models as foundations for "future state" planning scenarios.

However, managing a shared service is no easy task. Overseeing such an enterprise requires managing experts from multiple government agencies. A COE of this composition should also include leaders from the private sector to help ensure that the right channels are used for driving policies and implementation.

Research shows that the most critical components for building supply chain resiliency include:

- Real-time access to data on disruption effects

- Supply market intelligence with insights into mitigative actions

- Access to skilled experts who know what to do with this information

To strengthen the effectiveness and security of supply chains, agencies need to quickly execute decisions that drive actions, with a direct line to the right actors in each link of the supply chain. Developing these capabilities requires a combination of appropriate skills, supply risk technology, and communication channels that enable agile responses. Effective preparation cannot be taken for granted; supply chain readiness requires a defined process and a governance framework to analyze and respond, often based on limited options.

For these reasons, government-led, industry-involved shared service entity represents the most effective instrument for delivering capabilities to manage supply chain resilience.

```
┌─  ACTION STEPS  ──────────────────────────────────┐
│                                                            │
│   •  By taking advantage of synergies between agencies and industry partners, a   │
│      government-led shared service center of excellence can foster public-private  │
│      collaboration to diagnose, design, and sustain supply chains to              │
│      build resiliency.                                                             │
│                                                                                    │
└────────────────────────────────────────────────────┘
```

Diagnose the acquisition ecosystem

Governments should begin by diagnosing the entire acquisition ecosystem and identifying key vulnerabilities, critical supply risks, and suppliers impacted by these risks. This takes considerable time and effort, given the difficulties involved with managing diagnostic work among multiple agencies and numerous businesses, trade associations, and international partners.

Vulnerability and risk may be further complicated by context. For example, a life sciences manufacturer described how chip shortages and the low availability of reagents impacted the provision of COVID-19 tests. In terms of national security, vulnerability means understanding the nature of component shortages. One defense industry expert explained, "The Tier 1 supplier was not the problem. The issue was a Tier 4 and a Tier 5 connector that was not available. The lack of one inexpensive part prevented more than a dozen aircraft from being deployed."

A June 2021 report[3] issued by the White House identifies four major supply chains as especially vulnerable:

*   Semiconductor manufacturing and advanced packaging

*   Large capacity batteries for electric vehicles

*   Critical minerals and materials

*   Pharmaceuticals and active pharmaceutical ingredients

After identifying vulnerable categories, governments must develop a set of critical risks to monitor these products and services. For example, critical risks impacting semiconductor manufacturing include:

*   Fragile supply chains

*   Malicious supply chain disruptions

*   Obsolete semiconductors and related challenges to profitability

- Customer concentration and geopolitical factors

- Erosion of the U.S. microelectronics ecosystem

- Skilled worker shortages

- Intellectual property theft

- Capturing innovation benefits

- Aligning public-private interests

For governments, information sharing requires visibility into critical events, especially when national defense is involved. However, suppliers may hesitate to provide visibility to governments when warning about sustainment shortages for critical military systems. This inhibits the development of trusted customers and suppliers.

In addition, mergers and acquisitions may mean that prime vendors do not know who is in their supply network, leading to sudden disruptions when a component is no longer supported. In one case, a U.S. firm was acquired by a Chinese company, which meant that the acquired U.S. firm could no longer sell products to the U.S. government.

Another lesson learned was the importance of mapping supply chain networks to build effective supplier relationships. Machine-generated supply network maps may be inaccurate without validation. For this reason, network mapping needs organic verification based on source-level data.

Data is essential to reducing risks associated with supply chain disruption. However, data relevant to supply chains does not reside in most government systems. Commercial partners will need to be heavily involved in collecting key information.

ACTION STEPS

- Governments need to determine the areas of highest vulnerability to supply chain risks, and map their supply chain networks to recognize and build key supplier relationships that can address those risks.

Apply design thinking to develop key supply chain components

Design thinking can help governments build supply chain resiliency by developing statements of work, specifications, and sourcing networks with resiliency in mind. Effective networks must be designed at the outset of a program.

As governments build supply chain immunity in the face of shocks, they need to establish inventory stockpile requirements. Stockpiles apply not only to pandemic-related goods, but also to inventories of critical commodities such as energy, pharmaceuticals, semiconductors, aerospace components, and other national security products. Many government agencies can manage one-time disasters, but struggle with broader crises that shock supply chains daily.

Several government experts support the notion that "you will never stockpile your way out of disruption issues." To create agile domestic production capabilities at a cost-efficient price will require the further development of advanced manufacturing capabilities. However, this could run counter to national mandates, such as U.S. procurement practices that minimize cost at the expense of quality.

Stakeholder education will also be an important factor in network design. Typically, government program managers focus on cost, assessment, and scheduling. Adding supply chain resilience to these criteria would require a major shift in sourcing strategy.

This may include establishing pre-award intelligence requirements that require vendors to make business continuity plans transparent and provide location details about where materials are sourced. This change has been described as "democratization of data"—anyone working on a program can see the data and understand where disruptions may occur. To build supply chain immunity and resiliency, governments need to implement robust shared technology platforms for supply chain visibility and planning. These platforms need to include AI tools, data analytics, intelligent workflows, and supply chain mapping information to inform decision making and resource deployment.

Supply chain visibility also enables decision makers to pivot from a reactive to a predictive stance and mitigate problems before they occur. Real-time analytics and predictive modeling can support future-state planning. To develop this capacity, governments need to define a problem set and then identify the data needed to address that challenge. Supply chain visibility should occur in real time and provide transparency into the status of critical components and materials. To make sure users have total supply chain visibility, the private sector will also need to collect and share relevant data.

⎯ ACTION STEPS ⎯

- To design effective networks, governments need to establish inventory stockpile requirements, educate stakeholders to drive change, and develop technology for supply chain visibility and planning.

Sustain supply chains through risk mitigation and private sector partnerships

After establishing a visibility network and data collection protocols, a government-led supply chain shared service strategy can shift to a "sustain" mode. This includes the development of predictive models, mitigation strategies, and partnerships with private-sector organizations to innovate and expand capabilities.

Wargaming is a useful risk mitigation tool. These exercises bring together stakeholders from different functions to explore various scenarios and examine how future shocks to supply chains could impact government assets, leading to improved procurement approaches and local sourcing alternatives.

Supply chain wargaming also supports stockpile management. Participants discussed that the evolving concept of a "virtual stockpile," which enables distributors and manufacturers to hold materials within their own operations, but also provides data visibility to make these materials rapidly available to governments in a crisis.

With the growing sophistication of predictive analytical tools, governments can build on insights gained from wargaming to develop more accurate "what if" scenarios and contingency plans. Technologies such as AI and digital twins—the Port of Rotterdam uses digital twinning to visualize and make decisions quickly and effectively[4]—could also be used to find out where supply chains can break down under stress conditions.

To sustain supply chains, investments are required in resilience capabilities. However, many agencies lack the financial resources and authority to make these investments. Contract officers perennially weigh cost, schedule, and performance, often leading to trade-offs between operations and longer-term sustainment capability. Indeed, government procurement often drives other purposes and objectives, resulting in multiple goals and measures of success. Improving the resilience of government critical supply chains should be considered as a key requirement in procurement decisions, alongside product cost, life cycle costs, and environmental impacts.

Procurement also has a responsibility to act as an organized entity on the demand side. Clear demand signals create economic incentives to invest in strategic industries. These signals also increase the willingness to share data and share the development of more comprehensive business continuity plans.

Designating vulnerable industries as essential to a national economy may lead to additional challenges, such as steering investment into critical areas. This requires recognition of structural difficulties within domestic supply chains to meet economic and security objectives. If at-risk essential sectors cannot be sourced without higher costs, then governments need to invest in domestic industries that support national security, such as electric batteries, semiconductors, and pharmaceuticals.

To improve supply chain resiliency, governments must foster strong partnerships with the private sector. By sharing information and developing mutual trust, governments and businesses can help each other adjust to different situations that might arise in an unpredictable, disaster-prone world. The U.S. National Emergency Business Operations Center—part of the Federal Emergency Management Agency—has established a precedent for developing such partnerships.[5]

Measuring costs and return on investment also supports supply chain resilience. Governments often do not track these costs, nor costs related to expediting fees, emergency alternative sourcing, and overtime. And since financing often occurs through progress payments, costs are simply passed on to the government after being incurred—increasing overall costs in subsequent years.

ACTION STEPS

- To sustain a resilient supply chain, and better understand the potential impact of disruptions, governments should run war games, use predictive analytics, and improve acquisition strategies and private-sector partnerships.

Roundtable in Rotterdam, the Netherlands

For an international perspective on developing supply chain resiliency for governments, a roundtable event was held at the Port of Rotterdam in the Netherlands, where European experts added context to the action items introduced in Washington. The event was cosponsored by the American Chamber of Commerce in the Netherlands. The Port of Rotterdam—a very large government-owned entity, the largest seaport in Europe, and a key European supply chain hub—is embarking on a data-driven modernization strategy.

In the Dutch discussion, cooperation between governments and private industry emerged as essential in bringing the shared services concept to fruition. For example, the shipping industry has difficulty in obtaining and sharing data. Ports, supply chains, and transport networks each have their own API systems. In addition, governmental rules and regulations often prohibit the sharing of information between port operators and logistics providers. The ability of governments and commercial entities to exchange data on a timely basis needs to be a high priority task when building systems that support resilient supply chains.

Given the interest in recent advances in generative AI, the Rotterdam roundtable provided insights into the role that AI and other advanced technologies—such as automation and quantum computing—will play in supply chain resilience. Algorithms using these technologies have potential to optimize the operation of container-lifting cranes, direct vehicles, and help pilots bring ships safely into ports as busy as Rotterdam, which handled 467.7 million tons of goods in 2022.

However, these new technologies also represent potential risk. When discussing supply chain vulnerabilities, roundtable participants shared concerns about the security of supply chain networks. In the hands of hackers and absent strong cybersecurity protections, AI and quantum computing could disrupt logistics, customs operations, and border protection.

Roundtable participants agreed with the criticality of building security into the design of emerging technology systems to drive resiliency, rather than bolting on security only after a risk or threat arises. The Rotterdam roundtable provided insights into the benefits—and potential risks—that advanced technologies such as AI, automation, and quantum computing will have in transforming supply chain operations.

Modernize supply chains to build resilience

Building supply chain resiliency solutions starts with a strategy involving a government-led, industry-involved shared service and center of excellence. Given the central role of a shared approach to building supply chain resiliency, how can governments set up these collaborative organizations that meet their specific requirements? Though the recommendations outlined in this chapter were developed within a U.S. government context, this framework could also be applied to other democratic governments with similar agency structures.

In the U.S., a shared service for supply chain resilience could include multiple agencies that share a common objective. The European Union already has a similar framework that shares data and information among countries.[6] A shared service could span several domestic agencies with direct insights into various types of civilian and national security supply chain disruptions. These could include the Departments of Homeland Security, Commerce, Health and Human Services, Energy, Transportation, State, and Defense, as well as the Intelligence Community. Other nations may choose to house a shared services capability in ministries or bureaus with similar responsibilities.

ACTION STEPS

- Shared service capability needs to exist as a core responsibility, and the government should own it, lead it, and drive cross-border collaboration with other countries.

- Establish agency mission-support leadership roles for supply chain management that address cross-departmental and interagency component tasks.

LOOKING FORWARD

Assembling the multiple components of a supply chain resiliency solution will need more than government participation. The private sector will
also need to be involved when developing this capability. For this reason,
private-sector advisors to agencies should include business leaders and subject matter experts from different nodes in the supply chain. These experts
could come from equipment manufacturers, distributors, logistics providers,
hospitals, retail pharmacy chains, and drug manufacturers.

Governments are responsible to broad constituencies for building supply
chain immunity, and a shared services center of excellence provides a
practical structure to manage this responsibility. Such a strategy would
integrate the expertise of government agencies with private-sector business
acumen. It also provides the flexibility to anticipate and respond to
continuously changing supply chain disruptions.

Endnotes

1   The 2022 CEO Study. *Own your impact: Pathways to transformational sustainability.* IBM
    Institute for Business Value. May 2022, https://ibm.co/c-suite-study-ceo.

2   Handfield, Robert, and Daniel J. Finkenstadt, *Supply Chain Immunity: Overcoming our
    Nation's Sourcing Sickness in a Post-COVID World.* 2022. Springer, https://link.springer.
    com/book/10.1007/978-3-031-19344-6.

3   "Building resilient supply chains, revitalizing American manufacturing, and fostering broad-
    based growth." A report by The White House. June 2021, https://www.whitehouse.gov/
    wp-content/uploads/2021/06/100-day-supply-chain-review-report.pdf.

4   Boyles, Ryan. "How the Port of Rotterdam is using IBM digital twin technology to trans-
    form itself from the biggest to the smartest." IBM blog. August 29, 2019, https://www.
    ibm.com/blogs/ internet-of-things/iot-digital-twin-rotterdam/.

5   "National Business Emergency Operations Center Fact Sheet." Federal Emergency Man-
    agement Agency. May 28, 2019, https://www.fema.gov/sites/default/files/2020-03/nbeoc-
    fact-sheet _ 2019.pdf.

6   "Data Act: Commission proposes measures for a fair and innovative data economy." Euro-
    pean Commission press release. February 23, 2022, https://ec.europa.eu/commission/
    presscorner/detail/en/ip _ 22 _ 1113.

Chapter Four

Sustainability

INTRODUCTION

Building sustainability and climate resiliency into government institutions is more important than ever. The world's natural resources—including public lands—are integrally connected to our economy, health, environment, and society. Recent attention and investment in land management, water conservation, and energy generation and transmission—with a focus on how these factors translate into sustainable infrastructure—are creating opportunities to enhance climate resilience. Examples include the global 30-for-30 initiative, U.S. Great American Outdoors Act, and U.S. Bipartisan Infrastructure Act provisions for energy transmission and electric vehicles.

From a broader outlook, "climate and environmental risks are the core focus of global risk perceptions over the next decade—and are the risks for which we are seen to be the least prepared. The lack of deep, concerted progress on climate targets has exposed the divergence between what is scientifically necessary to achieve net zero and what is politically feasible."[1]

This chapter spotlights the critical importance of integrating sustainability and climate resilience strategies into our government institutions as climate impacts continue to mount. It focuses on three major topic areas: clean energy transition, sustainable development, and water management, offering practical insights and recommendations that governments can take advantage of in the near term to build climate resilience.

Setting Context

Sustainability is now top of mind among citizens, governments, and businesses. Recent research conducted by the IBM Institute for Business Value (IBV) finds that 68 percent of individuals across 33 countries say that environmental sustainability is very or extremely important to them.[2] Meanwhile, the IBV 2022 CEO study found that sustainability is the top business challenge identified by CEOs impacting their organization over the next 2-3 years. Yet, for all the talk and good intentions, progress has been limited. IBV research shows that while 86 percent of organizations have a sustainability strategy, only 35 percent have acted on their strategy. Moving the needle on climate resilience is proving very difficult.[3]

Source: The forthcoming IBM Center report, Integrating Climate Resilience, *by Chris Mihm—as well as informed by the Future Shock roundtable discussion and resources.*

But new opportunities are emerging. Data and digital technologies open new ways to drive change in priorities and practices. They can be infused into enterprise processes and decision making and drive improved environmental outcomes. Greater transparency and insight into climate conditions allow consumers, companies, investors, and governments to change the way they buy, produce, sell, transport, consume, and govern, which in turn has the potential to transform the way economies operate.

Building climate resilience entails substantial upfront investments and difficult trade-offs to achieve long-term sustainability. Still, through careful planning and broad public engagement, this transformation will demand a concerted effort by public, private, and societal actors. But after years where progress has been too limited, substantive change is within reach. The National Academy of Public Administration's Grand Challenge on Build Resilient Communities notes that "public agencies and administrators have an important role to play in building resilient communities. As this will require a crosscutting intergovernmental and intersectoral approach, public administrators can bring a diverse array of public, nonprofit, and private organizations together to develop strategies and implement programs. They can assist with mitigating and withstanding stresses, recovering, and applying lessons learned."[4]

Insights and Recommendations

The Future Shocks dialogues on climate resilience focused on three major topics:

- Clean energy transition

- Sustainable development (including land management)

- Water management

A broad cross-section of experts with experience at all levels of government, the private sector, civil society, academe, and international organizations recommend actions governments can take in the near term to build climate resilience across the three major topic areas. The identified steps do not constitute an exhaustive list of possible.

Strengthen capacity at the local level
All crises are local—but there is wide variation in how localities respond.[5] The impacts of climate disruption may be a global existential crisis, yet the effects are experienced differently across regions, communities, and individuals.

Local communities have vastly different capacities, needs, and risks that require differing types of resilience response. The roles and responsibilities among the federal, state, local, and tribal governments for resilience need to be clearly defined to ensure coordinated capacity development and guard against gaps. Communities need a better understanding of how to use federalism as an asset to develop flexible resilience governance models that work across the levels of government.

The differences in outcomes are often a product of political choices about what is important and will therefore receive priority attention and resources. Regarding resilience, differing capacities can result from decisions that reflect deep-seeded equity issues. Local resilience efforts must be the foundation of any effective national response. Since it is at the local levels that the varying effects of climate change are most directly felt, it is often easier to broker agreements on specific actions to be taken. A primary question is, therefore, how can local efforts best be supported, augmented, and incentivized given the many competing priorities they face and limited resources available?

Local governments could use additional support in identifying the variety of ways they can strengthen resilience. Local economic development incentives and zoning codes can be used to redesign living areas to consider the natural environment and the risk of climate disasters more fully.[6] Local government also can implement policies and programs designed to reduce energy consumption by creating systems and infrastructure that encourage non-wasteful solutions.

The point is not to suggest that these are new ideas—indeed they are being pursued with great success in many communities. In Europe and elsewhere, communities have demonstrated how climate adaptation can be integral to broader economic and local transformations leading to revitalized and more livable urban areas. Rather, the point is that information on how local policy and program tools can successfully be used singularly and more important in combination to foster resilience needs to be widely captured and disseminated.

Local resilience efforts often suffer from a shortage of knowledgeable staff—and those in place may be at the breaking point. For example, local emergency managers—whose responsibilities can span across multiple types of emergencies—are stretched way too thin. Multiple, overlapping "current shocks" that require immediate response are overwhelming their abilities to plan and respond.

Creative efforts are underway at regional, state, and local levels that are helping to build leadership and expertise on climate issues and resilience. For example, the Institute for Georgia Environmental Leadership (IGEL), formed in 2001, is an effort to build leadership capacity and working net-works at the state level.[7] According to IGEL, it provides annual leadership development programs and a collaborative network for participants to iden-tify and implement shared environmental solutions. Over 600 environmental leaders across all sectors in Georgia have participated in the program.

Local governments are recognizing that their resilience efforts need to be "whole of government" initiatives capable of cutting across local bureaucra-cies and organizing a collective effort in their jurisdictions. Designating Chief Resilience Officers (CROs) is one model increasingly being used to bridge organizational boundaries. "The Rockefeller Foundation launched the 100 Resilient Cities (100RC) program in 2013 to transform city governments, specifically by establishing the role of chief resilience officer—a senior leader in city government working to break down silos to build a more resilient city."[8] Building on these city efforts, some state-level CROs in the southeastern United States are now meeting informally to share information and experiences to mutually build capacity.

ACTION STEPS

- Work closely with local governments to understand specific capacity needs and how they can be met.

- Build communities of practice to develop local expertise in resilience planning and implementation.

- Share examples of successful local practices that have wider applicability, particularly in the use of local economic development incentives and zoning codes.

Build cross-boundary partnerships

Climate disasters and their spillover effects have no respect for geographic and political boundaries. Resilience initiatives likewise often need to cross jurisdictions to provide for coordinated efforts response and to share knowledge and experience. Regional partnerships to protect and enhance the Great Lakes, the Chesapeake Bay, and the Everglades are broad, multi-jurisdictional efforts.

Several examples illustrate the value of partnerships that bring together stakeholders across sectors to identify and address climate issues and the need to strengthen resilience. For example, the Southeast Florida Regional Climate Change Compact is an example of collaboration across local governments.[9] The Compact is a partnership between Broward, Miami-Dade, Monroe, and Palm Beach Counties in Florida. According to the Compact, it seeks to "work collaboratively to reduce regional greenhouse gas emissions, implement adaptation strategies, and build climate resilience across the Southeast Florida region." Its efforts center on sharing tools and knowledge, increasing support and political will, and coordinating action.

Also, the Ten Across (10X) initiative is certainly one of the geographically broadest regional collaborations.[10] The 10X initiative covers the U.S. I-10 corridor, which runs across the southern United States, from Los Angeles, California, to Jacksonville, Florida. According to 10X, "the U.S. Interstate 10 corridor (is) the premier observatory for the future, one which presents the challenges of the 21st century in their highest relief. Together with our growing network, we engage the conditions found within this transect to reveal our collective capacity to create a more resilient future."

Taking advantage of today's data availability and technology to analyze and share it on a greater scale than ever before is needed to achieve the substantial transformation and innovation required for sustainability. Digital technologies can enable a new model of sustainability governance where the private sector, governments, and local communities work in collaboration as partners.

ACTION STEPS

- Encourage regional collaboration that maps to cross-boundary climate risks.

- Use data to identify collaborations opportunities to avoid duplicative efforts and pinpoint gaps.

- Gather and share good practice on collaborations, particularly on the models employed and use of dashboards to manage performance.

Foster public engagement
Resilience planning almost inevitably requires balancing off competing interests and priorities. Water-related issues (floods from too much and droughts from not enough) provide countless illustrations of how contentious such issues can be, and how much needed progress can be stalled at key decision points. Experience has shown that the only way to equitable solutions is through community-based multistakeholder forums to discuss

and balance different interests. More broadly, however, resilience initiatives grounded in well-established public engagement strategies and human-centered design approaches offer proven paths for ensuring that voice, access, and representation are afforded to all segments of a community.

Government communication strategies need to continue to develop in sophistication and targeting. Risk and disaster communication are well recognized disciplines. However, governments at all levels need to do more in key areas, such as incorporating insights from behavioral science on how to structure choices into communication strategies. Communication strategies also need to speak to the public in a language that leads to action. For example, references to "100-year floods" may give a false sense of security rather than promote resilience efforts. Expanding the use of "compelling stories" in resilience communication can make the situation and calls for action less abstract and technical.

ACTION STEPS

- Encourage regional collaboration that maps to cross-boundary climate risks.

- Use data to identify collaborations opportunities to avoid duplicative efforts and pinpoint gaps.

- Gather and share good practice on collaborations, particularly on the models employed and use of dashboards to manage performance.

Manage climate risks and strengthening resilience

Risk management provides decision makers and the public with clear pictures of the risks and expected consequences from climate change, as well as the opportunities from improved resilience. Effective risk management also considers the synergies and "spillover" effects—both positive and negative—of resilience initiatives. For example, promoting walkable urban areas can have a host of major economic and social benefits that extend well beyond energy savings. On the other hand, rapidly moving to electric vehicles can further stress already overburdened electric grids. Identifying and understanding secondary effects is important so that they are effectively managed.

Risk must be continuously monitored and reassessed as needs change and response strategies evolve. According to March 2023 Intergovernmental Panel on Climate Change report, "the effectiveness of adaptation, including ecosystem-based and most water-related options, will decrease with increasing warming. The feasibility and effectiveness of options increase with integrated, multi-sectoral solutions that differentiate responses based on climate risk, cut across systems, and address social inequities. As adaptation options often have long implementation times, long-term planning increases their efficiency (high confidence)."[11]

ACTION STEPS

- Widely share information on the methodologies, technology, and data used in risk management.

- Fully consider the potential positive and negative spillover effects from resilience initiatives.

- Develop case studies and guidance on how specifically to use the results of risk assessments to inform planning and guide decisions.

Financing Climate-Related Sustainability and Resiliency Initiatives

There are two related ways to pursue climate change initiatives that focus on sustainability and resilience via direct funding and structuring investment incentives. As a major step forward, the 2021 federal Bipartisan Infrastructure Law (BIL) provided $550 billion through 2026 in federal funding for infrastructure, including roads, bridges, and mass transit, water infrastructure, resilience, and broadband. Moreover, federal R&D spending is vital in this area. Climate-related federal R&D funding is particularly important because much of the technology that will be needed to fully make the green energy transition is not currently available. The U.S. Department of Energy's Office of Clean Energy Demonstrations has been identified as an important development in accelerating the green energy transition.[12] The Office's programs include "investments in clean hydrogen, carbon management, advanced nuclear reactors, long-duration energy storage, industrial decarbonization, demonstrations in rural areas and on current and former mine land, and more." The BIL provided $21.5 billion to support large-scale clean energy demonstration projects.

The private sector can be a constructive partner in the transition to clean energy and strengthening resilience. Beyond the funding available through the BIL for projects undertaken by the private sector, a key task for government is to understand how to work with the private sector and to "get the incentives right" for broader private sector investments. "Public agencies at all levels of government have a role in funding clean energy R&D and spinning new technologies off to the private sector. These technologies can help reduce carbon dioxide emissions and mitigate climate change risks."[13] The Inflation Reduction Act (IRA) was acknowledged as a major step in creating the right investment incentives. In addition to tens of billions of dollars in direct spending, the IRA contains about two dozen tax provisions to incentivize the transition to green energy, with a special focus on equity issues.

There is also the need to better budget for risk, especially climate risks. Biden administration proposals show the budget and revenue implications of climate change across numerous categories for federal programs. For example, the FY2024 budget shows illustrative projections for increased expenditures under several climate scenarios.

ACTION STEPS

- Reinforce mechanisms that connect specific local resilience funding needs to public and private sources.

- Work with the private sector to understand how spending, tax policies, regulations, and government contracting can be used to incentivize private sector investments.

- Budget for climate risk.

Government's Role in Leading and Supporting the National Resiliency Agenda

The U.S. federal government has important and overlapping roles in leading, incentivizing, supporting, and facilitating state and local resilience initiatives. But to fulfill these roles, the capacity to direct and coordinate efforts across the federal government and with state and local governments needs to be strengthened.

Underscoring the need for action, the Government Accountability Office (GAO) issued its most recent biannual High Risk List on April 20, 2023.[14] Limiting the federal government's fiscal exposure by better managing climate change risks, first added to the list in 2013, remains on the 2023 list. GAO identified actions urgently needed in the federal government's roles as (1) insurer of property and crops, (2) provider of disaster aid, (3) owner or operator of infrastructure, (4) leader of a strategic plan to coordinate federal efforts, and (5) provider of data and technical assistance to federal, state, local, and private sector decision makers.

Climate change and resilience efforts obviously do not align neatly with governments' organizational silos. Such crosscutting problems require networked and sophisticated responses. These include organizing federal service delivery along the lines of "life experiences" rather than federal program structures and administrative processes. For instance, recovering from a natural disaster is one of the administration's targeted life experiences and human-centered design strategies are being used in the CX life experiences projects.

The federal government has broad experience with successful policy development through interagency collaboration, but much less so with interagency implementation. The evolving federal role in supporting resilience efforts increasingly requires the federal government to assume central roles in both policy and implementation. The implementation efforts of the Interagency Council on Homelessness, the federal Permitting Council, and Trusted Workforce 2.0, to reform the personnel vetting process, are examples of interagency implementation collaboration that provide models for federal efforts. In all cases, an implementation team with dedicated resources, a clear plan, and public performance dashboards are essential to their progress.

The federal government has a broad range of policy tools that it can use to spur resilience. For example, each year the federal government spends over $600 billion on contracts—and billions more are spent by state and local governments. This enormous buying power presents a powerful opportunity to change the marketplace if green energy, water and land management, and resilience are systematically embedded in procurement decisions and contracts.

The hundreds of billions of dollars in grants that the federal government sends to states and local government each year provide additional opportunities to incentivize and support resilience efforts. Grants programs that match state and local funding commitments are an example of using federal funds to incentivize and leverage state and local investments. Federal agencies also need to continue to explore creating grants that fund regional initiatives that cut across state and local boundaries. Funding for regional watershed protection is an especially ripe opportunity.

Grants requirements can also be used to create incentives for resilience. An example, GAO reported in 2019, is "requiring building codes and (design) standards based on the best available information for infrastructure built or repaired with federal funds."[15] The federal government should likewise aggressively use its grants and regulatory waiver authority to encourage experimentation and flexibility among the states and local governments. Waivers should come with clear performance standards and strong evaluation and reporting requirements to ensure that the bar is raised, and communities increase their resilience to climate disasters.

The federal government also should limit disincentives to resilience. Efforts to reduce the administrative burdens imposed on grantees need to be strongly encouraged. One way is to get the balance right on speed in the execution of grants, grantee flexibility, and financial and outcomes accountability. As part of this, federal efforts to support and incentivize local initiatives must be sensitive to vastly uneven capacity among localities.

While discretionary federal grants (i.e., those where the grantee must apply and be selected to receive the funding) constitute a subset of overall grant funding, such grants can be an important part of a government's resources. The problem is that many local governments, especially smaller ones, may lack the staff and the knowledge needed to apply for federal grants. Resource constrained local governments must carefully weigh the trade-offs of the time and effort needed to apply for a grant, the likelihood that their application will be approved, and the costs if it is not.

Agile regulatory processes also can be a key instrument in driving change and fostering resilience. In 2022, NAPA and the Project Management Institute presented an "agile regulatory framework" for federal agencies to use to streamline and reform their regulatory practices.[16] The administration has issued an Executive Order to modernize the regulatory review process.[17] Among other things, the order seeks to create a more transparent, inclusive, and publicly engaged regulatory process.

The federal government also has a central role in conducting and supporting research on climate change resilience. The federal government is best positioned to organize a national research agenda that identifies good practices across the public and private sector and how they can be scaled. The U.S. Climate Resilience Toolkit and the case studies it has gathered are a good example of information sharing that is intended to spur innovation.[18]

In addition, the federal government can facilitate innovation by compiling and broadly disseminating the results of state and local projects done under federal waiver authorities.

Finally, individual federal agencies that are most directly involved in resistance efforts need to ensure that their programs fully support local and regional resilience initiatives. For example, the U.S. Army Corps of Engineers' water infrastructure projects that address both water quantity and quality issues are major parts of successful local resilience water efforts.

ACTION STEPS

- Strengthen the federal capacity to support state and local resilience efforts.

- Use waivers—with rigorous evaluation requirements—to drive change and generate innovative approaches.

- Ensure federal procurements foster resilience.

- Reduce administrative burdens throughout the grants process.

- Create multistate, regional grant programs, especially for watersheds.

LOOKING FORWARD

Despite the clear evidence of the damaging consequences that climate change already is having on individuals and communities across the planet, the world is not on track to meet the internationally agreed-upon targets for limiting global temperature rise and transitioning away from the dependency on fossil fuels.

Governments at all levels need to continue to build capacity, create partnerships, share knowledge, and strengthen resilience strategies, including the transition to green energy, sustainable development, and water and land management.

While the benefits are large, building resilience can be costly and difficult. The challenge, as one expert noted, is governments and societies often do a much better job in addressing acute problems than they do with chronic problems. The chronic is always easy to postpone, given competing immediate priorities.

Endnotes

1   The Global Risks Report 2023, 18th Edition—Insight Report, World Economic Forum, January 11, 2023, https://www3.weforum.org/docs/WEF _ Global _ Risks _ Report _ 2023.pdf.

2   Balta, Wayne S., Manish Chawla, Jacob Dencik, Spencer Lin, *Sustainability as a Transformation Catalyst,* IBM Institute of Business Value, January 10, 2022, https://www.ibm.com/downloads/cas/N3RANMKO.

3   *2022 CEO Study—Own your impact: Practical pathways to transformational sustainability,* IBM Institute of Business Value, May 5, 2022, https://www.ibm.com/downloads/cas/6NJEKDD8.

4   "Build Resilient Communities." National Academy for Public Administration, blog post, https://napawash.org/grand-challenges/build-resilient-communities.

5   Barrett, Katherine, Richard Greene and Don Kettl, *Managing The Next Crisis: Twelve Principles for Dealing with Viral Uncertainty,* The IBM Center for The Business of Government, 2021, https://www.businessofgovernment.org/sites/default/files/Managing%20the%20Next%20Crisis _ 0.pdf.

6   For a vivid documentation on this point, see Donald F. Kettl, "The Storms That Test Local Governments," *Governing,* October 26, 2022, https://www.governing.com/community/the-storms-that-test-local-governments.

7   The Institute for Georgia Environmental Leadership (IGEL), https://igeleaders.org/.

8   Morales-Burnett, Jorge, and Rebecca Marx, The Rise of the Chief Resilience Officer: Lessons From 100 Resilient Cities, The Urban Institute, September 2022, https://www.urban.org/sites/default/files/2022-09/Rise%20of%20CROs%20Brief.pdf.

9   The Southeast Florida Regional Climate Change Compact, https://southeastfloridaclimate-compact.org/.

10   Ten Across (10X), https://10across.com/.

11   Intergovernmental Panel on Climate Change (IPCC). AR6 Synthesis Summary Report—Climate Change 2023, March 2023, https://www.ipcc.ch/report/sixth-assessment-report-cycle/.

12   https://www.energy.gov/oced/office-clean-energy-demonstrations.

13   "Steward Natural Resources and Address Climate Change", National Academy of Public Administration, https://napawash.org/grand-challenges/steward-natural-resources-and-address-climate-change.

14   GAO's High Risk program identifies government operations with vulnerabilities to fraud, waste, abuse, and mismanagement, or in need of transformation to address economy, efficiency, or effectiveness challenges. GAO reports every two years at the start of each new Congress, https://www.gao.gov/high-risk-list.

15   U.S. GAO, Disaster Resilience Framework: Principles for Analyzing Federal Efforts to Facilitate and Promote Resilience to Natural Disasters, GAO-20-100SP, October 2019, https://www.gao.gov/products/gao-20-100sp.

16   National Academy of Public Administration and the Project Management Institute, Agile Regulation: Gateway to the Future, June 2022, https://s3.us-west-2.amazonaws.com/napa-2021/Agile-Regulation-Gateway-to-the-Future-Report.pdf.

17   "Executive Order on Modernizing Regulatory Review," White House, April 06, 2023, https://www.whitehouse.gov/briefing-room/presidential-actions/2023/04/06/executive-order-on-modernizing-regulatory-review/.

18   U.S. Climate Resilience Toolkit, https://toolkit.climate.gov/steps-to-resilience/steps-resilience-overview.

Chapter Five

Workforce

INTRODUCTION

To address shocks and challenges, public agencies may need their workforce to have different knowledge, skills, and abilities than they have traditionally required. Amidst rapid technological changes and unprecedented industry disruptions, there is a growing disparity between the skills required in the workforce and the professionals who have obtained those skills. Public agencies will need to be able to recruit, retain, and develop a professional workforce who can successfully address these issues now and into the future, especially in critical areas like emergency preparedness and response, cybersecurity, supply chain, and transition to a cleaner environment.

This chapter points out that the public sector's traditional standardized approaches to recruiting, hiring, developing, and retaining talent no longer meet current and emerging needs. Practical near-term insights and recommendations are offered to help governments at all levels to create and sustain workforces needed to address current and future systemic shocks.

Setting Context

With an increase in the frequency of more challenging future shocks—which can include natural and human-made disasters, cybersecurity crises, and climate events, and more—there has never been a greater need for a skilled public-sector workforce. At the same time, governments increasingly use emerging technology to improve performance. Therefore, it is vital for many prospective employees to have expertise in using technological tools such as advanced robotics and artificial intelligence. In addition, workers will need to leverage cloud computing and big data, which will enable real-time data analysis to improve situational awareness.

The future workforce will also require skills in a variety of analysis, decision making, and communication in various media, including social media platforms. In addition, government entities need to hire more employees with skill sets in identifying and mitigating threats to physical and IT systems. Government entities are also in need of employees with expertise in risk management and research and development on innovation, as well as diverse skills from varied professional backgrounds ranging from engineering to modeling to telecommunications.

Source: The IBM Center blog post, Preparing Government Workforces for Future Shocks *(https://bit.ly/44YoZZe), by Chris Mihm—as well as informed by the Future Shock Roundtable discussion and resources.*

With an increase in the frequency of more challenging natural and human-made disasters, including cyberattacks, there has never been a greater need for trained emergency management professionals. As a result, governments are witnessing a vast expansion of emergency management roles across departments that did not have them previously. Unfortunately, many current emergency management professionals are burnt out after handling a slew of record-breaking disasters back-to-back. Therefore, it is imperative that governments build capacity to ensure these roles are being filled.

It is also no surprise that cyber threats against the public sector are on the rise, with 58 percent of state and local government organizations experiencing ransomware attacks in 2021—a 70 percent increase from the previous year. Furthermore, 59 percent of organizations reported an increase in attack volume and complexity over the last year, and 56 percent reported an increase in the impact of attacks. Yet, most government entities remain woefully unprepared to defend themselves against such attacks.[1]

To make matters worse, cybercriminals are constantly innovating, making it difficult for governments to stay protected. In addition, government agencies are the owners and users of highly sensitive data. Yet, shrinking IT budgets, a skills shortage, cloud adoption, and reliance on a wide network of contractors and third-party vendors widen the attack surface. It is imperative that these organizations step up their efforts to mitigate cyber events.

A plethora of skills are needed in the cybersecurity workforce. For example, government entities need to hire more employees to identify and mitigate threats to internal IT systems and networks. For this role, employees should have skills in cyber defense analysis, cyber defense infrastructure support, incident response, and vulnerability assessment and management. Government entities are also in need of employees who can build safer and more secure IT systems, which requires expertise in risk management, software development, systems architecture, and technology R&D.

A New Approach to the Workforce

The public sector's traditional standardized approaches to recruiting, hiring, developing, and retaining the needed talent no longer meet current and emerging needs. To cite just a few examples:

- The federal government's mission-critical skills shortages have been on the U.S. Government Accountability Office's (GAO) High Risk List since 2001, with only limited progress reported.

- Challenges in acquiring and retaining mission-critical skills can be particularly acute for state and local agencies involved in emergency preparedness and response. The diversity of the skill sets required, the need for surge capacity during emergencies, and the evolving missions of organizations to accommodate the overlapping nature of emergencies create additional staffing problems for preparedness and response.

- A separate cyber resilience roundtable sponsored by the National Academy of Public Administration and IBM concluded that to address the rapidly growing gap between supply and demand for cybersecurity professionals, "It is important to increase the cyber talent resource base and put it at the top of the list of actionable priorities. . . . cyber skill shortfalls impact a broad set of disciplines including analysis and engineering, software development, threat intelligence, penetration testing, auditing and consulting, digital forensics, and cryptography."

- Local governments are similarly challenged by skills gaps that undermine service delivery. As one example among many, the Berkeley City Auditor reported in June 2023 that "Berkeley had a high vacancy rate, reflecting staff shortages. These shortages have caused reductions in basic services for community members, such as delayed staff responses and facility closures."

Insights and Recommendations

To help government address these persistent and daunting workforce challenges, insights from the Future Shocks initiative offer recommendations of workforce strategies that governments need to develop and implement.

Systemically integrate strategic planning with workforce plans

It is important that agency leadership systemically integrate strategic planning with workforce plans as an integral way to acquire and develop talent
that meet current needs. Agencies should use a strategic approach that (1)
involves top management, employees, and other stakeholders, (2) identifies
the critical skills and competencies that will be needed to achieve current
and future programmatic results, (3) develops strategies that are tailored to
address skill gaps, (4) builds the internal capability needed to address administrative, training, and other requirements, and (5) monitors and evaluates the
agency's progress toward its human capital goals and the contribution that
human capital results have made toward achieving programmatic results.[2]

There is substantial value in using foresight strategies to understand future
talent needs. Strategic foresight seeks to look beyond the immediate horizon
and provide organizations and their leadership different views of the future
world—ones they may not have thought of or be comfortable with, but views
that are plausible, challenging, and impactful.[3]

Foresight strategies can be used as a complement to traditional planning
efforts, reframe the perspective of strategic planners, uncover potential blind
spots, and design a better long-term vision and plan a way forward that
meets all current workforce and human capital requirements. Talent management should be understood as a continuum, with the first step to identify
the talent required to meet current and emerging program needs. Agency
strategic planning should use insights from enterprise risk management and
strategic foresight to identify skills needed to address future shocks and other
emerging challenges. Data gathered from the process can assist workforce
planners and inform agencies in identifying and remediating potential workforce and skill gaps. Using foresight methods to address skills gaps further
enhances an agency's anticipatory culture.

ACTION STEPS

- Integrate workforce development into the strategic planning process putting
  emphasis on acquiring and developing talent.

- Leverage foresight strategies to understand future talent needs.

- Build an anticipatory culture and approach to the workforce
  development process.

Strengthen HR capacity while expanding participation in workforce development

Human resource office support is vital, but line managers must actively participate in recruitment, hiring, and training and development—not just leave this to human resource professionals to handle. It is critically important when building the next generation workforce to expand who participates in the workforce development process, and to have this relationship of trust continue throughout placement.

Organizations would benefit from strengthening the capacity and orientation of HR professionals to better support line managers in implementing innovative workforce strategies. Many HR offices suffer from critical skills shortages, while at the same time needing to build capacity to develop and use innovative workforce management tools.

HR offices should also more fully use existing personnel flexibilities while making evidence-based cases for greater flexibility when appropriate. Agencies often have a wide variety of workforce flexibilities and authorities—such as critical pay and hiring authorities—that can help to address skills gaps. However, they may not always know about or understand how best to use these tools.

ACTION STEPS

- Strengthen the capacity and orientation of HR professionals to better support line managers in implementing innovative workforce strategies.

- Expand who participates in the workforce development process to include HR professionals, program experts, and frontline managers.

Use agile approaches to workforce acquisition and development

Generative AI and other technological advances are rapidly and radically altering the nature of work. Many existing jobs and even some entire occupations may benefit from automation. Agile approaches can ensure that recruitment and hiring strategies take full advantage of technology and quickly pivot to acquire newly identified talent needs. Creating dedicated opportunities for continuous reskilling and learning to address emerging technologies are likewise vital.

Agencies can pioneer innovative learning opportunities by broadening outreach to academia and industry, identifying new opportunities for external assignments. Particularly in new technology and data-focused occupations, learning from academic labs and industry leaders offers new insight and a broader range of knowledge to each employee. Agencies can leverage internal centers of excellence and align training outcomes across their organization. Optimizing the balance between centralized training (e.g., leadership, collaboration, innovation) and decentralized training (skills-building, occupation-focused) will improve overall efficiency and accelerate employee development. Effective talent development incorporates new models of highly personalized and increasingly agile learning. Agency talent development for today's workforce should be more employee-centric, requiring more in-depth knowledge of employee potential and incorporating a wider range of learning and training opportunities. Training must be globally accessible and tailored to mission requirements.

All too often, the current recruitment approach overly prizes the "right" educational majors and "directly relevant experience." A skills-based approach, according to the Office of Personnel Management (OPM), "helps hiring managers focus on what candidates know how to do, not where they learned it. It values all relevant skills for the role at hand, whether they are learned in the classroom, on the job, or on one's own."[4] A skills-based approach opens opportunities for recruitment from a wider range of sources, helps build a diverse and resilient workforce, and minimizes unnecessary credentialism.

Government occupations often require deep technical knowledge. But they can also require skills beyond specific technical areas. These include softer skills such as teamwork, collaboration, communication with diverse communities, and discernment (the ability to separate the signal from the noise). Boundary spanners are needed—agile generalists who can build and integrate the work of specialists across disciplines and organizations.

ACTION STEPS

- Ensure recruitment and hiring strategies take full advantage of advances in technology.

- Create opportunities for continuous reskilling and learning to address emerging technologies.

- Pursue an employee-centric talent development strategy that incorporates new models of highly personalized and increasingly agile learning.

Establish a data strategy to guide decisions and transform workforce development

At the federal level, OPM has a 2023-2026 data strategy to harness workforce data and increase the value and use of federal workforce data. According to the strategy: "Given that OPM collects data on the federal civilian workforce across the employee lifecycle, from recruiting to employment to retirement, the agency has a historic opportunity to become a hub for delivering data-driven policy, enhanced analytics, data standards, and digital solutions that together are key enablers for strategic human capital management across the federal government."[5] Public-facing dashboards and metrics should be used to show progress and pinpoint improvement opportunities at all levels of government.

ACTION STEPS

- Build a strong, data-driven culture that increases data competencies enabling agencies to better harness the power of data in developing effective workforce policies, programs, and services.

- Leveraging data, automation, advanced analytics, and artificial intelligence technologies to enhance hiring and workforce development decision making.

Rebuild organizational cultures, operating models, and facilitate governmentwide collaboration

Agencies at all levels of government need to ensure that their organizational cultures are inclusive and welcome new hires with diverse backgrounds and skills. Too often new hires find that organizational cultures, processes, and tools do not align with their expectations—in which they may quickly leave for other employment. This is particularly the case when government technology lags private sector standards that new hires are accustomed to using.

Cross agency collaborative mechanisms can assist with developing policy, piloting new approaches, supporting implementation, and gathering and sharing good practices.

For example, the National Cyber Director established the National Cyber Workforce Coordination Group (NCWCG) and its subordinate working group, the Federal Cyber Workforce Working Group (FCWWG), in December 2022. The NCWCG serves as the principal interagency forum for federal agencies to address challenges and opportunities associated with cyber education, training, and workforce development, and serves as an implementation vehicle for the upcoming national strategy on cyber workforce and education. The FCWWG is the primary forum for interagency planning and executing necessary actions to build the federal cyber workforce and talent pipeline.[6]

The complex problems that governments seek to address span the boundaries of agency jurisdictions, levels of government, sectors, and professional disciplines. In direct response, how government leaders think about the workforce must span boundaries as well. For example, FEMA examines its "total force" with full-time FEMA employees at the center, but also including a wide range of other federal, state and local, private sector, and civil society partners with key roles in helping FEMA meet its disaster response mission.

ACTION STEPS

- Cross agency collaborative mechanisms can assist with developing policy, piloting new approaches, supporting implementation, and gathering and sharing good practices.

- Ensure that agency cultures are inclusive and welcoming to new hires with diverse backgrounds and skills.

LOOKING FORWARD

Advances in technology, changes in workforce demographics, and the resulting opportunities for new management approaches combine to shift the culture and landscape in which agencies operate in fundamental ways. In the IBM Center report, *Growing Leaders for Public Service*, Ray Blunt finds that growing the next generation of public service leaders stands as the most critical responsibility of senior public service leaders today—while among the most uneven and least understood efforts carried out across federal agencies. This goal of managing talent for tomorrow's needs goes to the heart of building the government workforce of the future.[7]

Agency leaders must build and manage a workforce that moves at the speed of change. The American people expect and deserve the best service from their federal government, which in turn requires a talented, highly skilled federal workforce drawn from a competitive pool. Gaps in digitally savvy and young talent highlight a critical need for governments to attract new skills and experiences from outside their organizations.

Endnotes

1   Mahendru, Puja, "The State of Ransomware in State and Local Government 2022," Sophos, Abingdon, United Kingdom, September 28, 2022, https://news.sophos.com/en-us/2022/09/28/the-state-of-ransomware-in-state-and-local-government-2022/.

2   GAO-20-129: INFORMATION TECHNOLOGY: Agencies Need to Fully Implement Key Workforce Planning Activities, Government Accountability Office (GAO), October 2019, https://www.gao.gov/products/GAO-20-129.

3   Developing & Applying Strategic Foresight for Better Human Capital Management Building a 21st Century Workforce in the Face of Plausible Futures, U.S. Office of Personnel Management, https://www.opm.gov/policy-data-oversight/human-capital-management/foresight-guide.pdf.

4   "Guidance Release—E.O. 13932; Modernizing and Reforming the Assessment and Hiring of Federal Job Candidates," Office of Personnel Management (OPM), Washington, D.C., May 19, 2022, https://chcoc.gov/content/guidance-release-eo-13932-modernizing-and-reforming-assessment-and-hiring-federal-job.

5   Data Strategy—Fiscal Years 2023-2026, U.S. Office of Personnel Management, Washington, D.C., March 2023, https://www.opm.gov/data/data-strategy/opm-data-strategy.pdf.

6   National Cyber Workforce and Education Strategy: Unleashing America's Cyber Talent, Office of the National Cyber Director, Executive Office of the President, Washington DC, July 31, 2023, https://www.whitehouse.gov/wp-content/uploads/2023/07/NCWES-2023.07.31.pdf.

7   Blunt, Roy, *Growing Leaders for Public Service*, The IBM Center for The Business of Government, Washington D.C., Second Edition, August 2004, https://www.businessofgovernment.org/sites/default/files/BluntReport3.pdf.

PART II | BUILDING RESILIENCE: PREPARATION AND RESPONSE

Chapter Six

Eight Areas for Government Action

By Chris Mihm

INTRODUCTION

In Part I, we discussed how the unprecedented number and scope of catastrophic events have stressed governments, businesses, communities, and individuals. These shocks range from the global COVID-19 pandemic, supply chain disruptions, and debilitating cyberattacks, to weather extremes such as deadly heat waves, "100-year floods," and raging wildfires.

These cascading, disruptive events have raised fundamental questions about what capacities governments need to anticipate, prepare for, and respond to crises.

Clearly, these shocks have no respect for geographic, jurisdictional, political, or organizational boundaries. Adaptation, preparation, and response cannot be the sole responsibility of one sector, one program, one agency, or one level of government. Rather, the key to success—and the root cause of many failures—is the capabilities of the individual network participants and the strength of the network before, during, and after a shock through partnerships established between sectors, levels of government, and agencies. Simply put, complex problems cannot be solved in silos.

What specific and practical steps can governments take in the near term to better prepare and respond to catastrophic events? The research and roundtable discussions of the Future Shocks initiative, which framed recommendations for action in each of the five domains, also reflected a number of crosscutting themes regarding capacities that can help strengthen the public sector preparation for and responses to major events yet to come.

Part II summarizes and elaborates on these common themes, identifying action steps in eight areas as described in Figure 1, that governments at all levels can take to anticipate, prepare for, and respond to shocks of any type. The steps and related practices that follow do not constitute an exhaustive list of actions, but rather reflect discussions from the roundtables and related research.

As a central conclusion, the underlying capacities of governments need to be significantly augmented across these eight actions in two interrelated ways:

- Improve working relationships and alignment among network partners in governments, the private sector, civil society, and the public.

- Strengthen the capabilities to operate successfully in a networked environment.

The overarching goal of building these capabilities is to position governments to become more resilient in the face of inevitable future shocks.

Figure 1. Eight Areas for Government Action

Improve Relationships and Alignment Among Network Partners
• Build a future shocks governance mechanism • Develop plans to mitigate crosscutting shocks • Manage risks and extend opportunities • Increase public participation and improve communication
Strengthen Capabilities to Operate Successfully in a Networked Environment
• Fast-track government innovation and transformation • Support data-driven decision-making strategies • Dedicate the right resources, and get the incentives right • Invest in a future shock-ready workforce

Shocks: Disruptive Events Defined

Shocks are events with severely disruptive consequences. They could be rapid- or slow-onset, or regional or global. While the scope and nature of a particular shock can vary, each requires governments to be prepared to coordinate a response (see Figure 2).

Shock events typically begin locally, and their impacts spread rapidly through contamination or contagion to societies and economies. Regional shocks are limited to a specific geographic area or sovereign state(s), and include events such as climate-related or other natural disasters, armed conflict, and cyber events/attacks on economies or critical infrastructure.

Rapid-onset shocks, such as wildfires, have immediate impacts requiring urgent action. Slow-onset shocks, including environmental risks resulting from climate change, provide more time for impacted governments and societies to adjust, react, and mitigate impact.

Figure 2. Speed of Government Response and Scope of Coordination for Future Shock Events

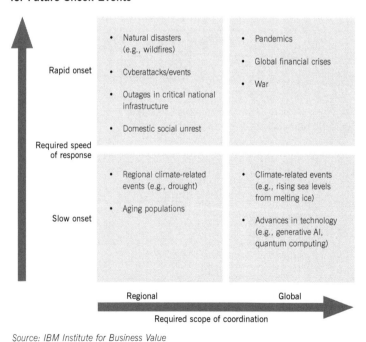

Source: IBM Institute for Business Value

Improve Relationships and Alignment Among Network Partners

Action 1. Build a Future Shocks Governance Mechanism

A 2021 IBM Center report, *Managing the Next Crisis: Twelve Principles for Dealing with Viral Uncertainty*, acknowledges that the key is networks—but they do not spontaneously organize themselves. That is, a successful network is not merely defined or mapped out on a chart, but also must include a governance approach that is consciously selected and used to actively manage.

Experience shows that there is no one right governance mechanism for organizing a network and responding to future shocks that require the active involvement of many partners across sectors. And in practice, mechanisms are often used in combination.

Significant and consequential breakdowns in cross-organizational collaboration have been well documented. These range from the response to Hurricane Katrina in 2005 to overwhelming public health systems during the COVID-19 pandemic. But a set of practices associated with successful network governance has emerged that can be adopted irrespective of the specific governance mechanism that is employed.

As discussed in Chapter 3 of Part I, a Center of Excellence is an ideal form of engagement to build supply chain resiliency, which could operate as a shared service. To garner multiagency support and cross-sector collaboration for quick response, a shared service emerged as an ideal form of engagement to build supply chain resiliency.

The Federal Emergency Management Administration (FEMA) strives to adopt a whole community approach that "attempts to engage the full capacity of the private and nonprofit sectors—including businesses, faith-based and disability organizations, and the American public—in conjunction with the participation of state, local, tribal, territorial, and federal governmental partners."[1]

Using Memoranda of Agreement (MOAs), continuous training, tabletop exercises and simulations, and "wargaming," network participants can define and reinforce roles, responsibilities, and working relationships across the network. Jointly coordinated capacity development among localities, mutual aid agreements, regional compacts, and financial incentives for localities to build their capacity can also facilitate the ability to respond to future shocks.

Ultimately, successful networks result from preexisting organizational—and at least as important, personal—relationships based on familiarity and trust.

The Southeast Florida Regional Climate Change Compact is an example of collaboration across local governments.[2] The Compact is a partnership between Broward, Miami-Dade, Monroe, and Palm Beach Counties in Florida. According to the Compact, it seeks to "work collaboratively to reduce regional greenhouse gas emissions, implement adaptation strategies, and build climate resilience across the Southeast Florida region."

Future shocks are often global crises. It is therefore not surprising that coordination and information sharing extends across national boundaries. For example, C40 Cities is a global network of mayors from about 100 major cities committed to cutting their own emissions, limiting global warming, and "building healthy, equitable, and resilient communities." C40 Cities include close to 600 million people and have about one-fifth of the global economy.

Designating a lead official to coordinate efforts across organizations is an often-used model to lead networks. At the federal level, these officials are often referred to as "Czars" for their program or policy area. Local governments are recognizing that their resilience efforts need to be whole-of-government initiatives capable of cutting across local bureaucracies and representing a collective effort in their jurisdictions. Designating chief resilience officers (CROs) is one model increasingly being used to bridge organizational boundaries.

In building the network, government planners should recognize that private and nonprofit involvement is much more than merely helpful or additive—it can determine the success of the response to a future shock. These organizations collectively bring resources, community relationships, capacities, and agility that governments may lack.

The roundtables observed that networked approaches to addressing future shocks requires a cultural change for many organizations. Working across sectors with differing values, legal frameworks, operating models, and accountability mechanisms is not easy.

The cyber roundtable provided a vivid illustration of the challenge and the need to break organizational cultural silos. Threat actors are developing new technologies quickly to penetrate networks and thwart efforts to contain threats, which can be difficult to counter when those efforts depend on coordination across entities with differing standards, missions, and priorities.

Action Steps

- Create networks of key partners and stakeholders to address future shocks that cut across government agencies and the private sector.

- Select a network governance mechanism that fits the purpose of the network and the nature and scope of the shock to be addressed.

- Establish the network's implementation approach the defines leadership, roles, responsibilities, and accountability before a shock occurs.

- Build ongoing relationships and trust to minimize misunderstandings and confusion during a crisis.

- Strengthen the capacities of the network and its individual participants through, for example, joint exercises and knowledge sharing.

- Recognize and seek to address structural and organizational cultural barriers that limit collaboration.

Action 2. Develop Plans to Mitigate Crosscutting Shocks

The IBM Center's October 2022 report, *Eight Strategies for Transforming Government,* observed that "(P)erformance management initiatives over the past two decades helped shift the conversation within and across U.S. government agencies—from a focus on measuring program activities and outputs to a focus on achieving mission outcomes This refocus represents a fundamental shift in thinking, acting, and managing within the public sector, away from a focus on process and on what one needs to do, to a focus on benefits and ensuring the desired impact of government programs."[3]

This fundamental shift is particularly important—and difficult—in addressing shocks that cut across agencies, levels of government, and sectors. It is more important because crosscutting shocks require crosscutting responses that align efforts not only of federal agencies, but of a vast patchwork of other actors as well. In this sense, outcome-oriented future shock strategic planning must be national in orientation and not merely federal. As a positive step forward, as of March 2023, The National Cybersecurity Strategy's five pillars and related strategic objectives constitute a plan for national cyber resilience and not merely federal.

Strategy mapping and strategy management-at-scale is a tool that can be used for planning to address crosscutting issues. As the 2023 report for the IBM Center, *Addressing Complex and Cross-Boundary Challenges in Government: The Value of Strategy Mapping,* explains that new techniques and processes are needed to make sense of the challenging situations involving complex, interconnected issues in which multiple organizations must make contributions to make the changes needed to effectively confront the challenge.

Mapping strategies to manage change

"Strategy mapping is a technique to help leaders across multiple levels, organizations and/or sectors understand the system in need of change and articulate the interventions needed to bring about the desired changes. Strategy mapping helps users visualize the cause-and-effect chains in a system and the actions that can be taken to change the system. Mapping process itself functions as a shared intellectual framework and backbone to help guide the effort. It facilitates negotiation and commitment to agreements about what to do, how to do it, and why; and then communicates strategies in a way that is easily understood and acted upon. It provides a framework, for guiding, monitoring, reviewing, and evaluating strategy implementation."[4]

Developing a national strategy to strengthen the cyber workforce is a strategic objective under the national cybersecurity strategy. The objective demonstrates that workforce plans to acquire and develop talent needed to meet current and future needs should be fully integrated with mission-related strategic planning.

Action Steps

- Create whole-of-government, or even whole-of-society, strategic plans to address future shocks.

- Rely on documented successful practices in developing these network-wide plans.

- Align individual agency plans, goals, performance measures, and strategies with network-wide strategic plans.

- Leverage technology, including AI, to facilitate decision making.

- Integrate management capacity considerations, such as workforce talent needs, into strategic plans.

Action 3. Manage Risks and Extend Opportunities

Risk management provides decision makers and the public with insights on the risks and expected consequences from future shocks as well as the opportunities from improved resilience. The tools, techniques, and methods for risk management are well established and internationally accepted standards exist. However, the nature of risk management takes on new dimensions—and importance—in responding to future shocks.

The IBM Center's report on *Eight Strategies for Transforming Government* identified the nature of the challenge, noting that today's risk landscape requires a unified, coordinated, disciplined, and consistent approach, no longer focused on risk management as a compliance exercise or perceiving risks solely as problems to avoid. Research is needed in reconceiving risk management as a value-creating activity integral to strategic planning, decision making, and organizational resiliency.

Data driven modelling using generative AI and other tools, such as dashboards, is essential to understand the evolving and interconnected future shocks and their multifaceted consequences.

In addition, the U.S. federal government has a central role fostering consistency in risk management across all members of a future shock network. For example, the cyber roundtable observed that a seemingly isolated cyber event can escalate quickly into a full blown national or even global crisis, which underscores the need to prioritize standard cyber risk assessment frameworks to facilitate more efficient collaboration.

The federal government can also assist other organizations, particularly localities, in strengthening their own risk management programs. Local communities have vastly different capacities, needs, and risks that require differing types of responses to future shocks. As Katherine Barrett, Richard Greene, and Don Kettl noted in their IBM Center report, *Managing the Next Crisis: Twelve Principles for Dealing with Viral Uncertainty*: "All crises are local—but there is wide variation in how localities respond."[5]

Finally, risk must be continuously monitored and reassessed as risk evolves and risk appetites and response strategies change. The feasibility and effectiveness of options increase with integrated, multi-sectoral solutions that differentiate responses based on climate risk, cut across systems, and address social inequities. As adaptation options often have long implementation times, long-term planning increases their efficiency.

Action Steps

- Establish a dedicated approach to risk management that recognizes the ever-evolving future shock risks and responses.

- Ensure risk management is deeply embedded in all strategic and operational decisions and does not become a stand-alone, compliance driven exercise.

- Focus on how addressing future shocks can create opportunities for a better future and not only the negative consequences of a shock.

- Use data-driven modeling, generative AI, and other tools to assist in all aspects of risk management.

- Standardize risk assessment frameworks across the network.

- Establish federal leadership for overall risk assessments and share results and methods and provide technical assistance across the network.

Action 4. Increase Public Participation and Improve Communication

The Edelman Trust Barometer has documented a crisis in trust in government over the last decade. Lack of trust stems from multiple causes. The most worrisome might be the inability of most governments and politicians around the world to cast a credible vision for the future—one that would be rooted in ethics and enabled by competence, accounting for the challenges and fears experienced by constituents.[6]

Clarity of message based on evidence and data, and rapid response to disinformation are essential elements of effective decision making. Unfortunately, the wicked nature of most shocks virtually guarantees that multiple "sources of truth" will emerge that can lead to confusion, a lack of trust, and disjointed decision making.

Broad public participation can help to guard against what scholar E. Lisa F. Schipper has referred to as "maladaptation"—adaptation efforts that are not genuine improvements and may even increase vulnerabilities. According to Professor Schipper, "More deliberate, inclusive planning could introduce ideas for adaptation strategies that outsiders have not even thought of. Local participation, development, and implementation will give individuals more of a stake and help bring about successful outcomes."[7]

Governments at all levels need to improve the way they communicate about future shocks. This begins with recognizing that different parts of a community have vastly dissimilar needs and capabilities during an emergency. For example, physical or financial barriers, pressing medical needs, disabilities, and fears of relocating are among the reasons people may not evacuate from harm's way during a climate disaster.

Reinforcing resilience with generative AI

Along with corporate executives, the leaders of governmental organizations are closely following the development of generative AI and how this technology is transforming the workplace. During the next 12 months, 38 percent of government leaders report in the IBV survey that generative AI will moderately or significantly impact workplace capabilities. During the five years, 93 percent of them expect that generative AI will moderately or significantly impact workplace capabilities.

Although adaptation is in the early stages, at least four use case scenarios are emerging where generative AI could significantly contribute to how governments prepare for and respond to shock-level disruptions. These applications include:

* Automated budgeting by analyzing spending patterns, forecasting needs according to trends, and improving how decision makers allocate resources

* Expedited citizen services by using natural language processing to respond to inquiries faster through pre-programmed answers and directing inquiries to the most appropriate agencies and departments

* Enhanced decision making by using predictive analytics to deliver insights based on historical data points and current conditions, enabling government leaders to make informed decisions beyond experience or intuition

* Optimized emergency response through the analysis of large data sets to predict and respond to emergencies more effectively, helping agencies allocate resources more efficiently during crisis situations

Communication strategies must also be adapted to reach the different populations, considering what information is communicated, how it is communicated, and by whom. This entails identifying and working closely with trusted voices in the community to send messages that will be understood and accepted.

Communication strategies also need to speak to the public in a language that leads to action. The key is communication that prompts action on future shocks. It must strike the right and difficult balance between making the shock real and personal while not contributing to inaction, either due to despair because the problem is seen as overwhelming or apathy that the shock is just a new normal that we all must learn to live with.

Governments need to promote building awareness in education systems from an early age. The participants suggested establishing multi-sector partnerships, including with academia, to develop more robust curricula on sustainability from K-12, community colleges, and higher education.

Efforts to address future shocks should not reinforce existing inequalities. For example, it is widely recognized that those communities contributing the least to the climate crisis tend to suffer the most from climate disasters. Overcoming trust deficits, based on historical mistreatment and neglect, requires active listening, sensitivity, and a genuine commitment to address relevant concerns.

Action Steps

- Understand the great challenges posed by public distrust in government and disinformation on efforts to address future shocks.

- Create robust opportunities for public participation at all stages— planning, response, recovery—of efforts to address future shocks.

- Ensure those opportunities are inclusive of all parts of the community and create genuine avenues for voice, access, and representation for all.

- Carefully design communication strategies using trusted voices, storytelling, and other approaches that lead to public understanding and effective actions.

- Building age-appropriate awareness of future shocks into the education curricula.

Strengthen Capabilities to Operate Successfully in a Networked Environment

Action 5. Fast-Track Government Innovation and Transformation

Emergent and unanticipated events and future shocks no longer fit within organizational structures, work processes, and cultures. Future shocks will not wait for governments to react according to official priorities and prerogatives. Rather, leaders in government need to create cultures and processes that continuously improve competence and innovation throughout their organizations.

As the world has emerged from the depths of the COVID-19 pandemic, most countries are seeking to build the resilience needed to better respond to crisis. Cristina Caballe Fuguet, Tim Paydos, and Mike Stone noted in the IBM Center's 2022 report *Emerge Stronger and More Resilient: Responding to COVID-19 and Preparing for Future Shocks* many governments, even those caught off-guard by the pandemic, quickly shifted to rapid innovation and modernization. They suggested that fostering rapid innovation and agility will be a core theme as governments prepare for inevitable future shocks.

No single approach works in all circumstances, but a central part of the solution is applying insights from agile software development to the full range of policy and program domains. Agile is defined as a "new management paradigm, (where) the top priority is 'customer' or end-user satisfaction. Small teams do the work in multiple short periods of time. Individuals operate within a focused set of networks. Innovative tools and working approaches that facilitate innovation and support problem solving are used. Risk is identified and addressed early. And the focus is on doing, not documenting."[8]

Agile methodology prioritizes end-user satisfaction. Laudable efforts are underway to organize federal service delivery along the lines of "life experiences," such as recovering from a natural disaster and facing a financial shock, rather than federal program stovepipes and administrative processes. Human-centered design approaches are major aspects of efforts to reduce the administrative burden of program participation on recipients.

Fully embracing AI and other technological advances must be a cornerstone to build resilience to future shocks. For example, the government of India "introduced an electronic vaccine intelligence platform (CoWIN) that has improved the efficiency of vaccine registration, immunizations, and appointments throughout the country. Since CoWIN's deployment in January 2021, more than 1.1 billion people have been vaccinated against COVID-19 across more than 5,000 sites—most of which were in rural and hard-to-reach areas."[9]

Supporting leaders and innovators with agile methods[10]

- **Agile leaders need an agile mindset.** A willingness to try new ideas and processes to achieve better results.

- **Integration is critical to execution.** The elements described in the framework are designed to work together.

- **Leaders at all levels need to analyze and understand trust in and across their organization.** Trust is key for employees, the public, and partners.

- **Agile government must begin with understanding customers.** The customer experience and journey starts with the customers are, how their journey with the organization flows, what constitutes "defining moments" in their experience.

- **Public values must be respected, and the public must be engaged.** Focus on openness, integrity, and fairness, which can improve overall trust.

- **Networks should form the default development and implementation pathway wherever possible.** Collaborative networks can be internal, external, international, and should serve as a force multiplier for mission execution.

- **Cross-functional teams should drive integrated solutions to problems.** Cross-functional teams bring more perspectives and encourage diversity of thought, greatly enhancing the chances for success.

- **Appropriate speed and persistent iteration will enable the organization to shape and reshape successful approaches.** Setting aggressive deadlines to accomplish work and demonstrate continual achievement builds internal and external support.

Action Steps

- Drive innovation throughout the organization because traditional program approaches are inadequate in an era of cascading future shocks.

- Expand the use of agile management methodology.

- Put citizens, customers, and program recipients at the center through human-centered design and make concerted efforts to reduce administrative burdens.

- Manage the disruptive potential of AI and other technologies while harnessing their tremendous potential.

Action 6. Support Data-Driven Decision-Making Strategies

Decision makers at all levels and the public require high quality and cred-ible data to guide decisions. The IBM Center report, *Emerge Stronger and More Resilient: Responding to COVID-19 and Preparing for Future Shocks*, points out that public sector leaders must build a robust analytic founda-tion for increasing situational awareness, predicting potential policy impacts, and providing citizen transparency. In this way, data serves as the new raw material that institutions need to mine and refine to rebuild trust.

Successful networks seek agreement on key elements of a data strategy well before an emergency occurs. For example, they seek consistency in definitions for data elements from across the network, agreement on what data will be needed in real time—including data disaggregated to offer insights on how future shocks are affecting different populations—and how it will be collected, how privacy will be protected, and how data will be made available to those who need it in formats they can readily use. The network's data strategy also includes a technology assessment to determine where gaps in technology need to be filled.

Designing and implementing a data strategy across a network is extremely challenging. For example, the Pandemic Response Accountability Commit-tee (PRAC), made up of 10 federal Offices of Inspectors General, attempted to track federal COVID relief funding. Looking at a small subset of all fund-ing, the PRAC reported in July 2023 that "Tracking pandemic funds to the community level required the use of multiple federal, state, and local data systems, and ultimately, we had to contact state and local entities directly to gain a better understanding and fill data gaps. In the end, complete data was either unavailable or insufficient and did not allow (PRAC) to definitively identify the total funding provided to the six communities (studied)."[11]

Given the often wide range of data and its diverse sources needed to address a future shock, strong privacy and confidentiality protections need to be built in from the outset. This is important to guard against the inap-propriate disclosure of sensitive and confidential business, personal, govern-ment operational, and classified data.

Overall, even the best data are valuable only to the extent that it is used to help guide decisions. The roundtables suggested that public-facing dashboards and metrics should be used to show progress, pinpoint improvement opportunities, and provide transparency to the public.

The federal government also has a central role in conducting and supporting research on future shocks. For example, the climate resilience roundtable participants said that the federal government is best positioned to organize a national research agenda that identifies good practices across the public and private sector and how they can be scaled. The U.S. Climate Resilience Toolkit and the case studies it has gathered are a good example of information sharing that is intended to spur innovation.[12]

Action Steps

- Create a data strategy—what data will be collected, by whom, when, where it is to be stored and reported, level of quality, how it is to be used—well before a crisis occurs.

- Disaggregate data to provide a comprehensive understanding of how a future shock will affect all parts of a community.

- Build in privacy and confidentiality safeguards.

- Encourage network participants to be forthcoming in reporting, especially in cases where they may perceive it is not in their interests to do so.

- Provide transparency through public reporting and public-facing dashboards.

- Use data to inform decisions, for example through learning agendas.

Action 7. Dedicate the Right Resources, and Get the Incentives Right

Future shocks can be mass casualty events and impose significant economic losses to individuals, organizations, and communities. Since 1980, the cumulative costs of major disasters (at least $1 billion in cost) in the U.S. are over $2 trillion.[13] Further, IBM reported in its annual *Cost of Data Breaches* report for 2022 that the cost of data breaches to organizations have reached an all-time high, to over $4.5 million per breach.[14]

Given these significant costs, the National Cybersecurity Strategy calls for a fundamental shift in how the United States allocates roles, responsibilities, and resources in cyberspace. This includes increasing incentives to favor long-term investments into cybersecurity. One of the Strategy's five pillars is to shape market forces to drive security and resilience.

The federal government has a broad range of policy tools that it can use to incentivize and support future shock resilience. For example, each year the federal government spends over $600 billion on contracts. Billions more are spent by state and local governments. This enormous buying power presents a powerful opportunity to embed future shock resilience in procurement decisions and contracts.

The need to improve the resilience among the nation's 130 million commercial and residential buildings illustrates how the federal government can spur needed action. Building codes are generally a local responsibility. However, the U.S. Government Accountability Office's (GAO) reported in 2019 on potentially "requiring building codes and (design) standards based on the best available information for infrastructure built or repaired with federal funds."[15]

The federal government should likewise aggressively use its grants and regulatory waiver authority to encourage experimentation and flexibility among the states and local governments. The federal government also must limit disincentives to resilience. Efforts to reduce the administrative burdens imposed on grantees need to be strongly encouraged. Local governments, especially smaller ones, often lack the staff and the knowledge needed to apply for federal grants. Resource constrained local governments must consider the time and effort needed to apply for a grant, the likelihood of approval, and the wasted costs if it is not.

The National Academy of Public Administration, in its *Grand Challenge on Steward Natural Resources and Address Climate Change*, observed, "Public agencies at all levels of government have a role in funding clean energy R&D and spinning new technologies off to the private sector. These technologies can help reduce carbon dioxide emissions and mitigate climate change risks."[16] The private sector can—and wants to—be a constructive partner in the transition to clean energy and strengthening resilience.

The governments need to improve budgeting to reflect risk. However, building resilience to cyberattacks, supply chain disruptions, climate disasters, and other shocks will be costly and difficult. The challenge, as one expert noted, is that we do a much better job in addressing acute problems than we do with chronic problems. When immediate priorities dominate the agenda, it is easier to put off chronic concerns until another time.

The problem is that many local governments, especially smaller ones, may lack the staff and the knowledge needed to apply for federal grants. Resource constrained local governments must carefully weigh the trade-offs of the time and effort needed apply for a grant, the likelihood that their application will be approved, and the wasted costs if it is not. The federal government should likewise aggressively use its grants and regulatory waiver authority to encourage experimentation and flexibility among the states and local governments.

There is the need for governments to better budget for risk. While the benefits are large, building resilience to cyberattacks, supply chain disruptions, climate disasters, and other further shocks be costly and difficult. The challenge, as one expert noted, is we do a much better job in addressing acute problems than we do with chronic problems. The chronic is always easy to postpone until another day, given competing immediate priorities.

Action Steps

- Use the full range of the tools of government including direct spending, procurement, grants, R&D funding, tax incentives, regulations, and others to support and incentive initiatives to address future shocks.

- Recognize the uneven capacities among local governments and other grantees by streamlining grants procedures and reducing administrative burdens.

- Promote the use of grant and regulatory waivers—with appropriate safeguards and outcome reporting—to enhance flexibility to address the differing local manifestations of future shocks.

- Budget for future shocks by continuing to increase the explicit recognition of future shocks risks in government budget processes.

Action 8. Invest in a Future Shock-Ready Workforce

Persistent mission-critical skills shortages are undermining the abilities of governments to meet their missions. The public sector's traditional standardized approaches to recruiting, hiring, developing, and retaining the needed talent no longer meet current and emerging needs. For example:

- The federal government's mission critical skills shortages have been on the GAO's High Risk List since 2001 with only limited progress reported.

- U.S., state, and local governments have lost more than 600,000 workers between the start of the pandemic and June 2022, affecting their ability to maintain basic services as well as respond to critical situations.[17] The overwhelming stress faced by frontline workers and first responders—who in many cases are themselves survivors of the disaster—underscores the importance of attention to burnout as well as the physical and mental health and well-being of staff.

- The cyber resilience roundtable concluded that "(T)o address the rapidly growing gap between supply and demand for cybersecurity professionals, roundtable participants stressed the importance of increasing the cyber talent resource base and putting it at the top of the list of actionable priorities."

The point made about private sector organizations in the IBM research insight, *The Enterprise Guide to Closing the Skills Gap: Strategies for Building and Maintaining a Skilled Workforce*, applies equally well to government: "As business platforms mature and companies continue to introduce new intelligent workflows to succeed on those platforms, the need for continuous reskilling in the workforce will be paramount to remain competitive. Hiring alone is not a sustainable solution to the talent crisis."[18]

Fortunately, the Academy's "No Time to Wait" reports[19] provide a path forward on tackling government's talent deficits. The Academy panel recommended the establishment of a competency-based talent management model that:

- Identifies the core competencies of occupational and professional groups

- Trains employees in the competencies they will need, and certifies the skills they bring

- Creates flexible teams matching competencies to missions

- Fosters continuous learning through occupational and professional communities of practice

- Reskills the government's workforce to match mission requirements with employee skills and ensures that these skills keep up with hyper-fast mission changes

Too often new hires find that the organizational cultures, processes, and tools do not align with their expectations—in which they may quickly leave for other employment. This is particularly the case when government technology is not up to the best private sector standards that new hires are accustomed to using.

Many human resource offices are suffering from their own critical skills shortages while at the same time needing to build capacity to develop and use innovative workforce management tools. For example, agencies often have a wide variety of workforce flexibilities and authorities—such as critical pay and hiring authorities—available that can be used to address skills gaps. However, they may not always know about or may not understand how best to use these tools.

The complex future shocks governments seek to address span the boundaries of agency jurisdictions, levels of government, sectors, and professional disciplines. In direct response, how government leaders think about the workforce must be boundary spanning as well.

Action Steps

- Develop strategies to address current mission-critical skills gaps.

- Support the health and well-being of first responders.

- Use scenario planning and strategic foresight to identify skills that may be needed as future shocks continue to evolve.

- Commit to continuous learning and reskilling.

- Recruit and develop skills across agencies, levels of government, and sectors.

- Expand the use of skills-based hiring to create a diverse workforce.

- Foster inclusive organizational cultures to make full use of new talent.

- Build the capacity of human resource offices by filling existing shortages and to serve as a strategic partner to line managers.

- Seek transparency over workforce issues so that any critical skills weaknesses in the network can be identified and addressed.

LOOKING FORWARD

Adopting New Ways to Think, Operate, and Collaborate

Societies and their governments face escalating and increasingly interrelated shocks that place enormous stress on communities and citizens. As isolated events quickly metastasize into mega-crises, governments must prepare for, respond to, and recover from these shocks, and develop the strategies to meet the mission. The key is not only to maintain a vulnerable status quo or adjust to an unsatisfactory "new normal", but also to build more equitable and sustainable governments and societies.

The crosscutting nature of shocks are challenging governments to adopt new ways to think, operate, and collaborate. This will require new organizational cultures that embrace agility, expand beyond bureaucratic boundaries, and attract and retain talent that can thrive and capitalize on transformative technologies such as generative AI.

In short, a government entity will need to be as impactful, broad-based, and fast-changing as the complex shocks it will need to address.

Governments must build sustainability in an era of profound disruption—but also in an era when resources for resilience are becoming more sophisticated. Taken together, the actions outlined in this chapter provide practical insights and options governments can use to be ready for the next future shock—now gathering on an unforeseen, but inevitable timetable.

Top five resilience-building priorities of government executives

1. Invest in technology and infrastructure to enhance communication and output.

2. Develop plans and strategies to respond to emergencies and crises effectively.

3. Ensure strong and adaptable governance structures to make timely decisions and lead effectively during crises.

4. Invest in workforce upskilling and training to increase efficiency and productivity.

5. Promote sustainability and adopt renewable energy sources to prepare resources for the future.

Chris Mihm, *PhD, is an Adjunct Professor at Syracuse University, teaching graduate courses on public administration and democracy and performance management. He is the former Managing Director for Strategic Issues at the U.S. Government Accountability Office where he led GAO's work on governance, strategy, and performance issues. He is also a fellow and former Board Chair of the National Academy of Public Administration.*

Endnotes

1   "A Whole Community Approach to Emergency Management: Principles, Themes, and Pathways for Action." FEMA. FDOC 104-008-1. December 2011. https://www.fema.gov/sites/default/files/2020-07/whole_community_dec2011__2.pdf.

2   The Southeast Florida Regional Climate Change Compact, https://southeastfloridaclimatecompact.org/.

3   Chenok, Daniel J., G. Edward DeSeve, Margie Graves, Michael J. Keegan, Mark Newsome, and Karin O'Leary, EIGHT STRATEGIES: for Transforming Government, IBM Center for The Business of Government, Washington, D.C., 2022. htps://www.businessofgovernment.org/sites/default/files/Eight%20Strategies%20for%20Transforming%20Government_1.pdf.

4   Bryson, John M. with Bill Barberg, Anne Carroll, Colin Eden, Bert George, Jose J. Gonzalez, Jessica Rochester, Laure Vandersmissen, and Bishoy Zak, *Addressing Complex and Cross-Boundary Challenges in Government: The Value of Strategy Mapping*, IBM Center for The Business of Government, Washington, D.C., 2023.

5   Barrett, Katherine, Richard Greene and Don Kettl, *Managing The Next Crisis: Twelve Principles For Dealing With Viral Uncertainty*, The IBM Center for The Business of Government, 2021.

6   Harary, Antoine, 2023 Edelman Trust Barometer: Rebuilding Trust Demands Articulating a Credible Vision for the Future, January 26, 2023. https://www.edelman.com/trust/2023/Trust-barometer/rebuilding-trust-demands-articulating-credible-vision-future.

7   Schipper E. Lisa F., "Maladapted Ill-conceived attempts at climate adaptation threaten to make a bad situation even worse," OpenMind Magazine, July 14, 2022. https://www.openmindmag.org/articles/maladapted.

8   Building an Agile Federal Government: A Call to Action. White Paper, The Project Management Institute, National Academy of Public Administration (NAPA), Washington, D.C., 2020.

9   Digital solutions for improved vaccine access, United Nations Development Program —Indonesia, November 22, 2022. https://www.undp.org/asia-pacific/stories/digital-solutions-improved-vaccine-access.

10   DeSeve, G. Edward, *The Future of Agile Government*, The IBM Center for The Business of Government, Washington, D.C., 2022.

11   *Tracking Pandemic Relief Funds that Went to Local Communities Reveals Persistent Data Gaps and Data Reliability Issues*, Pandemic Response Accountability Committee, July 2023. https://www.pandemicoversight.gov/media/file/practracking-pandemic-relief-fundsimpact-phase-i2pdf.

12   https://toolkit.climate.gov/steps-to-resilience/steps-resilience-overview.

13   "Billion-Dollar Weather and Climate Disasters." National Centers for Environmental Information, National Oceanic and Atmospheric Administration. October 2022. https://www.ncei.noaa.gov/access/billions/.

14   *Cost of a Data Breach Report 2023*. Ponemon Institute and IBM Security. July 2023. https://www.ibm.com/reports/data-breach.

15   U.S. GAO, Disaster Resilience Framework: Principles for Analyzing Federal Efforts to Facilitate and Promote Resilience to Natural Disasters, GAO-20-100SP, October 2019. https://www.gao.gov/products/gao-20-100sp.

16   National Academy for Public Administration (NAPA), Grand Challenges: Steward Natural Resources and Address Climate Change. https://napawash.org/grand-challenges/steward-natural-resources-and-address-climate-change.

17   Brey, Jared. "Government Worker Shortages Worsen Crisis Response." Governing: The Future of States and Localities. October 3, 2022. https://www.governing.com/work/government-worker-shortages-worsen-crisis-response.

18   LaPrade, Annette, Janet Mertens, Tanya Moore,and Amy Wright. *The enterprise guide to closing the skills gap: Strategies for building and maintaining a skilled workforce.* Research Insights: IBM Institute for Business Value (IBV). September 11, 2019.

19   Kettl, Donald, Doris Hausser, Jozef Raadschelders, Ronald Sanders, Stan Soloway, Joshua Gotbaum, Doris Hausser, Sean O'Keefe, No Time to Wait, Parts 1 & 2: Building a Public Service for the 21st Century, National Academy of Public Administration, Washington D.C., July 2017 and September 2018. https://napawash.org/academy-studies/no-time-to-wait-part-2-building-a-public-service-for-the-21st-century.

PART III | **ON FUTURE READINESS: INSIGHTS FROM EXPERTS**

INNOVATION

Chapter Seven

AI Literacy: A Prerequisite for the Future of AI and Automation in Government

By Ignacio F. Cruz
Northwestern University

INTRODUCTION

With the rapid progression of artificial intelligence and automation technologies, the public sector is in a state of transformation. Government leaders and managers are on the frontlines, responsible for harnessing AI's potential into tangible results. Numerous public efforts have been made to address AI's design, deployment, and maintenance, such as establishing the National Artificial Intelligence Initiative[1] and the Blueprint for an AI Bill of Rights[2] developed by the White House Office of Science and Technology Policy (OSTP). These pragmatic advancements aim to guide AI use across agencies and create a system for documenting use cases and principles. But one key assumption often underpins these developments—that stakeholders already have a comprehensive understanding of what AI is and how it can be leveraged across their workflows.

A new focus has emerged: cultivating strategy to enhance AI literacy. Originating from computer science, information studies, and learning sciences, AI literacy involves understanding the technical facets of AI and learning how to leverage it in practice. In a study from the Georgia Institute of Technology, researchers define general AI literacy as "a set of competencies that enable individuals to evaluate AI technologies critically; communicate and collaborate with AI; and use AI as a tool."[3] The push for more explainable, responsible, trustworthy, and transparent AI has been part of this shift. AI literacy requires not just learning but *learning to learn*—asking the right questions to comprehend how AI systems work. This requires understanding a tool's capabilities, its limits, ethical implications, and how to incorporate it into operations.

Blueprint for Building AI Literacy

This chapter delves into the vital role of strategic actions for AI literacy, particularly for leaders and managers navigating the intricacies of an increasingly automated workplace. It outlines a three-phased approach outlined in Figure 1. for boosting AI literacy, presenting key actions and practices to make government organizations more responsive and fundamentally reshaping them to deliver exceptional public services and achieve mission success. By adopting these strategic actions for AI literacy, governments can ensure that ongoing advancements in AI and automation are harnessed effectively and ethically, providing the greatest possible benefit to the public. This approach offers a crucial tool for government leaders and managers, helping them navigate the complexities of AI implementation within their organizations.

Figure 1. Blueprint for AI Literacy

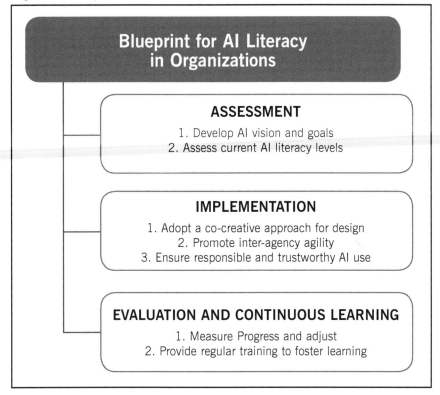

Assessment Phase

Develop AI vision and goals

The initial step in enhancing AI literacy within an organization involves establishing clear, actionable goals. These objectives should be tailored to the
unique needs of each organization, reflecting their specific context and use
cases for AI. For instance, one organization might focus on understanding
how AI can augment efficiency in routine tasks, while another might concen-
trate on understanding the ethical implications of AI in handling sensitive data.

Leaders are responsible for ensuring these goals align with the organization's mission, values, and strategic objectives. For instance, if a pillar of an
organization's mission is to enhance customer service, an AI literacy goal
could involve understanding how automation can be deployed for improved
client interaction and engagement. When establishing AI goals, organizations
should also consider potential challenges associated with AI integration, such
as data privacy, ethical use, and technical capacity. For example, a team

handling sensitive data might prioritize learning and mitigating privacy risks associated with an AI tool. Similarly, other teams with limited technical expertise might focus on building fundamental conceptual knowledge before using more advanced technology applications. These goals should be flexible and evolve alongside technological change and organizational growth.

The term 'AI' covers a broad spectrum including: algorithms, machine learning models, generative AI, recommender systems, neural networks, robotics, design principles, and industry trends. Acknowledging this diversity is crucial as leaders define AI's role within their organization and set corresponding literacy goals. The spectrum of learning should also be considered in the goal-setting process. Achieving AI literacy is a progressive journey, and goals can span a continuum, from understanding basic AI concepts and applications to comprehending more complex aspects—such as deciding the amount of risk arising from automating high-reliability decisions.

Given the emergence and widespread adoption of new forms of AI like generative AI, encompassing technologies like ChatGPT, Bard, and GitHub Copilot, leaders have the opportunity to consider how to define and set AI literacy goals. This shift involves more than just understanding AI's mechanics and using it responsibly. For instance, generative AI fosters dynamic user interaction, paving the way for creating new content and solutions to complex problems. Notably, this technological advancement is democratizing AI usage, transforming users from being primarily consumers of AI outputs to active creators with AI. In this context of rapidly evolving technology, the value of developing robust, flexible frameworks for AI literacy is key. Even as technologies change, the processes to comprehend, use, and enhance them remain crucial. Therefore, AI literacy goals must be conceptualized as dynamic and adaptive, ready to accommodate these evolving forms of interaction with technology. This will ensure that workforces are well-prepared for the future.

Assess current AI literacy levels

With goals outlined, the subsequent step is to assess the current state of AI literacy across different levels in an organization. This assessment forms an essential baseline, shedding light on existing AI understanding within leadership and illuminating areas requiring enhancement. AI literacy benchmarks play a vital role here, providing a well-defined standard against which the organization's AI knowledge can be evaluated. These benchmarks serve as a roadmap, guiding the organization to identify gaps, set realistic improvement targets, and track progress over time.

A significant part of AI literacy is developing data literacy as a competency. Data literacy refers to reading, understanding, creating, and communicating data as information. In the context of AI, this means understanding how AI systems collect, process, and interpret data. It also involves maintaining relationships with vendors to ask the right questions and unravel the complexities of these processes to ensure data literacy principles become embedded into tools.

However, the knowledge of AI and data should not be the endpoint. Leaders should decide where AI fits within the organization's operational framework. This can be achieved by conducting an audit of the existing workflow, identifying tasks that could be automated, processes that might face disruption and opportunities for new AI-enabled processes. If feasible, conducting internal surveys, interviews, or focus groups can offer invaluable insights during this assessment phase. The information gathered outlines the current state of AI literacy and aids in creating tailored educational programs. These programs should address the organization's leaders and managers' specific learning needs and knowledge gaps.

In addition to the technical aspects of AI, a human factors perspective plays an integral role in successful AI adoption. AI literacy assessments should evaluate employees' attitudes toward automation technologies. Understanding these sentiments can highlight potential barriers to AI acceptance and indicate any areas of resistance stemming from the organization's culture. The insights from this evaluation could help in developing communication adoption strategies and training programs that address these apprehensions. Further, it could help identify potential 'intelligence officers' or 'translators' within the organization. These specialists understand a tool's technical details and its potential application across various organizational departments. They serve as a bridge between AI specialists and operational staff to communicate how technology initiatives can contribute to larger organizational practices and goals. By integrating these human factors into AI literacy assessments, leaders can foster an environment that supports a more complete, inclusive transition toward AI adoption.

Implementation Phase

Adopt a co-creation approach for AI implementation
A co-creation strategy in AI implementation is indispensable for effective technology integration within organizations. This process is characterized by a back-and-forth dialogue between developers and end-users of AI technologies. A case study led by Stanford University in the healthcare sector provides an example.[4] Two machine learning tools—predicting potential

bed shortages and estimating patient readmission rates—were developed through an iterative co-creation process between developers and employees in a health system.

In the context of government agencies, the co-creation process might include several elements. First, developers and operational managers collaboratively identify potential AI solutions that align with the agency's needs and technical capabilities. Then, these proposed solutions are refined through continuous engagement with a broader group of stakeholders, including other department leaders or external experts. A prototype of the AI tool is then implemented on a pilot basis, allowing end-users—in this case, managers and staff—to provide real-time feedback and identify potential discrepancies or areas of improvement. The final stage involves refining the tool based on user feedback, adjusting the AI models, and ensuring the tool is both user-friendly and effective.

By fostering and practicing collaborative design, this approach can enable employees and leaders with a shared responsibility for the development of a tool, which is created collectively through practice and aims to address an employee's workflow. This co-creation process can be an opportunity for building trust and task-technology ownership among staff. As employees become involved in the development and refinement of AI tools, they can gain a deeper understanding and appreciation of the technology. This can help alleviate apprehension and resistance, promoting acceptance and successful integration of AI across operations.

Promote interagency agility

Building a future with successful AI integration necessitates collaboration and awareness, not just within a single organization but across a broad network of agencies. As leaders engaging with and leveraging these interagency connections is critical.

One key practice involves sharing each organization's AI use cases, challenges, and solutions with other agencies. The National Artificial Intelligence Initiative encourages this dialogue by requiring federal agencies to annually report an inventory of how they use AI in tasks and to share the database with other government agencies and the public.[5] This becomes increasingly relevant as a survey by Accenture reported that 76 percent of leaders across 16 industries struggle with understanding how to maximize AI value across operations.[6] Such a knowledge exchange serves as a platform for learning from others' experiences, facilitating the adoption of proven strategies, and unveiling potential uses of AI.

Leaders can both contribute to and benefit from a shared repository of knowledge and experience. This approach relies on a process of social influence, a concept rooted in social psychology, where peers' shared experiences and successes can positively impact the likelihood of wide-spread technology adoption. By championing inter-agency collaboration and fostering an internal culture of AI awareness, both an organization and the broader government network can be better positioned for successful tech-nology adoption.

Ensure responsible and trustworthy AI use

The responsible usage of AI, characterized by elements that include fair-ness, transparency, privacy, and explainability, is paramount when integrat-ing this technology into government operations. Yet, responsible use is only one side of the coin. Trustworthiness is another critical aspect, referring to the dependability of AI in producing accurate, consistent outputs under a wide range of circumstances. Ethical guidelines for AI use must be incorpo-rated into organizational policies and procedures, enabling leaders to make informed and ethical AI-related decisions. For example, the Department of Defense's five principles of AI ethics—responsibility, equity, traceability, reli-ability, and governability—provide a strong foundation. This involves a thor-ough understanding of the technology, rigorous testing of AI capabilities, and implementation of systems to detect and mitigate unintended consequences.

Trustworthy AI requires systems to be versatile and reliable, functioning cor-rectly under various situations and consistently delivering on their intended functions. This entails rigorous testing and quality assurance processes that scrutinize the system's performance. Trustworthy AI also emphasizes the reproducibility and verifiability of results. Auditability is a critical facet to achieving these principles. It involves the ability to develop processes to inspect and review the workflows the AI model employs to make decisions. This enables accountability and transparency in AI operations. Moreover, a significant aspect of trustworthy AI includes providing redress mechanisms. If the AI system makes an error, it is crucial to have procedures in place for affected parties to seek remedy or correction.

A principle that binds responsible and trustworthy AI together is user over-sight. While delegating decisions to AI systems can increase efficiency, users must retain control and the ability to intervene when necessary. This serves as a safeguard, ensuring that technology serves human-centric values and ethical norms. Several collaborative initiatives are shaping this area, under-lining the importance of broad stakeholder input. For instance, the National Telecommunications and Information Administration (NTIA) actively seeks feedback from various agencies to inform policies that support the develop-ment of AI audits, assessments, and certifications, thereby promoting trust in AI systems.[7] Similarly, the National Institute of Standards and Technology (NIST) has established the Trustworthy and Responsible AI Resource Center as a platform to foster trustworthiness in designing, developing, using, and evaluating AI products, services, and systems.[8] At both the state and federal levels, these collective efforts provide leaders with resources for developing ethical AI guidance.

AI systems can reflect and amplify societal biases and potentially lead to unfair outcomes. Moreover, the vast quantities of data collected and processed by AI systems pose a significant target for cyberattacks, data breaches, and misuse. Ensuring responsible AI use is an ongoing, complex, yet crucial task. It requires collaboration across all organizational levels and roles—whether from the intelligence officer who anticipates potential issues, the technical specialists who troubleshoot problems, or the operations personnel who implement the solutions. Each person, no matter their role, must have some form of AI literacy. This unified approach underscores the importance of everyone having a stake in understanding and managing AI technologies.

As leaders, being aware of these challenges and using existing frameworks, or developing new ones as necessary, is an essential part of this task. In addition to implementing ethical guidelines, organizations should also establish mechanisms for monitoring and reviewing the use of AI. This involves regular auditing and evaluations to ensure that AI systems are operating as intended and ethical standards are being upheld. This broad and cooperative approach ensures a thorough, organization-wide commitment to responsible and trustworthy AI use.

Evaluation and Continuous Learning Phase

Measure progress and adjust

Developing a generalized blueprint for AI literacy poses a unique challenge given the diversity of agencies, each with its distinct needs, resources, and regulations. However, a critical and shared step involves regularly assessing progress toward AI literacy goals and subsequent adjustments. Regular tracking can be achieved through follow-up assessments, feedback sessions, or performance reviews. Progress measurement should also consider qualitative aspects, such as employees' confidence and comfort in using AI tools, their understanding of AI's capabilities and limitations, and their efficacy in making informed decisions with their tools. These measures not only provide insight into the learning curve but also identify areas for improvement or adjustment in strategy. Achieving AI literacy is not a static goal but a dynamic, ongoing process. The feedback collected during this stage is invaluable for refining strategies, and ensuring that learning initiatives remain effective, relevant, and aligned with the organization's AI literacy goals.

Provide regular training and foster learning

Maintaining AI literacy necessitates fostering an environment of continuous learning. Leaders should ensure regular training sessions through various partnerships with universities, industry experts, and specialized in-house training initiatives. These partnerships provide leaders and managers with access to the latest AI developments and trends.

Creating an AI-literate culture is a strategic move that contributes significantly to the acceptance and effective use of AI technologies. This can involve organizing awareness campaigns, seminars, and workshops that not only demystify AI's black box, but also illuminate the potential of AI in enhancing public service delivery. Leadership plays a pivotal role in embedding this culture within the organization. By educating their teams about AI's capabilities and implications through various learning initiatives, they ensure to leverage AI strategically.

LOOKING FORWARD

Advancing AI Literacy

The strategic actions outlined in this chapter form a comprehensive approach to enhancing AI literacy within government operations. These actions—including setting clear goals, assessing current AI understanding, implementing technology through a co-creative approach, promoting inter-agency awareness, ensuring responsible use, and fostering a culture of continuous learning—are all key elements in this transformative process. Building a future where AI and automation enhance government operations and resonate with an AI-literate workforce requires a concerted effort from all stakeholders. The emphasis on AI literacy signifies a shift in mindset towards viewing emerging technologies not as mere tools, but as a strategic partner in enhancing public service delivery.

Ultimately, this three-phased approach aims to equip government leaders and managers with the insights and actions necessary to navigate the complexities of AI integration. Furthermore, these strategies can empower leaders to discern the potential of new tools confidently, paving the way for informed decisions about adopting and integrating cutting-edge technologies. By fostering an environment where AI literacy is at the forefront of organizational strategy, government agencies can become more efficient, responsive, and ultimately, advance their mission for the citizens they serve.

Ignacio F. Cruz is an Assistant Professor of Communication at Northwestern University. His research focuses on the Future of Work, specifically how organizations strategically design, implement, and assess emerging technologies in their workflows.

Endnotes

1   National Artificial Intelligence Initiative Office, "Legislation and Executive Orders," 2023, https://www.ai.gov/legislation-and-executive-orders/.

2   White House Office of Science and Technology Policy (OSTP), "Blueprint for an AI Bill of Rights: Making Automated Systems Work for the American People," 2022, https://www.whitehouse.gov/ostp/ai-bill-of-rights/.

3   Long, Duri and Brian Magerko, "What is AI Literacy? Competencies and Design Considerations," in Proceedings of the 2020 CHI Conference on Human Factors in Computing Systems (Association for Computing Machinery, 2020), 1-16, https://doi.org/10.1145/3313831.3376727.

4   Singer, Sara J., et al., "Enhancing the Value to Users of Machine Learning-Based Clinical Decision Support Tools: A Framework for Iterative, Collaborative Development and Implementation," Health Care Management Review 47, no. 2 (2022): E21-E31, https://journals.lww.com/hcmrjournal/Abstract/2022/04000/Enhancing_the_value_to_users_of_machine.11.aspx.

5   National Artificial Intelligence Initiative Office, "AI Use Case Inventories," 2023, https://www.ai.gov/ai-use-case-inventories/.

6   Accenture, AI: Built to Scale Report, 2019, https://www.accenture.com/us-en/insights/artificial-intelligence/ai-investments.

7   National Telecommunications and Information Administration, "AI Accountability Policy Received Comments," 2023, https://ntia.gov/issues/artificial-intelligence/ai-policy-assurance/received-comments.

8   National Institute of Standards and Technology, "Trustworthy & Responsible AI Resource Center," 2023, https://airc.nist.gov/Home.

Chapter Eight

Design Principles for Responsible Use of AI to Enhance CX Through Public Procurement

By Ana-Maria Dimand, Boise State University,
and co-authors Kayla Schwoerer,
Andrea S. Patrucco, and
Ilia Murtazashvili

INTRODUCTION

Government agencies are increasingly turning to artificial intelligence (AI) tools such as machine learning, chatbots, and generative AI to enhance customer experience (CX) and meet federal mandates for service improvement. While these tools offer significant opportunities to enhance public services and customer interactions, they also pose challenges,[1] including bias, discrimination, and unauthorized data access. Addressing these challenges requires strategies that extend beyond conventional management practices and necessitates a comprehensive policy framework.

This chapter explores the service delivery process, including the systems, people, and processes that indirectly influence CX. It highlights the pivotal role of the procurement process in acquiring and implementing ethical and responsible AI tools that enhance CX. It proposes two ways that public procurement processes can improve CX through AI, and presents seven design principles to guide the procurement of AI tools in the public sector. Overall, addressing these policy issues and incorporating the proposed design principles into a comprehensive AI policy framework can unlock the potential of AI in public procurement, thereby enhancing CX, building public trust, and advancing agency missions.

The Complexity of Customer Experience

CX is sometimes viewed as a mere public encounter between a government representative and citizen at a specific point in time. Such a view masks the complexity of CX, missing insight into how agencies can contribute to a truly exceptional experience. Therefore, two core ideas guide our consideration of CX.

First, CX includes the entire service delivery process, encompassing not only the initial experience but also the culmination of systems, people, and processes that work together in the provision of public services. Second, the notion of the "customer" cannot be limited to individual citizens, residents, taxpayers, or beneficiaries of government programs and services, as there is a diverse range of "customers" involved in public service provision. Most significantly, CX depends on organizations that benefit from public programs and services, which means that vendors and suppliers can also be considered customers.

Embracing the complexity of CX means acknowledging that CX involves meeting individual and organizational needs to advance organizational missions, improve service, and build trust. Therefore, customer-centric approaches to public service delivery must consider a more holistic perspective that acknowledges each stage of the process and its influence on the customer's perception, satisfaction, and experience.

From this holistic perspective, AI can play a key role in delivering a great CX. AI tools can improve service delivery, decision making, and policy in several ways. For example, AI's ability to collect and analyze large amounts of data can help agencies tailor and personalize public services and communications. AI-powered chatbots and virtual assistants can provide quick and accurate responses to customer inquiries, reducing wait times, and improving CX. AI can also contribute to good governance by providing customers with greater transparency and insights into government decision-making processes, thereby promoting public trust.

Deploying AI to Improve Customer Experience through Procurement in the Public Sector

Public procurement holds a pivotal role in ensuring the availability of essential goods and services for public service delivery, including AI technologies. This role is twofold, with procurement processes both contributing to the deployment of AI and benefiting from the use of AI.

First, procurement processes serve as the primary avenue for acquiring AI technologies.[2] As such, procurement offices act as "gatekeepers" for the procurement, influencing the implementation and management of AI systems. They assess and select credible vendors that supply responsible and ethically designed AI systems. This gatekeeping role ensures that the procured AI technologies are designed and implemented in a way that respects ethical guidelines, promotes transparency, and is user-friendly.[3] For instance, procurement agencies can incorporate performance metrics related to user experience and customer satisfaction into contracts and RFPs. Also, this encourages suppliers to develop innovative solutions that meet agency specifications and enhance customer experience. This contributes to a positive CX by building trust in AI systems, making their decision-making processes understandable, and ensuring that the systems are easy to use and helpful for internal users and also external stakeholders (such as citizens).

Second, AI tools can directly support the procurement process in the public sector.[4] This support manifests in two distinct ways: **operational efficiency** and **strategic decision making**.

On the operational front, AI can facilitate efficient and effective public procurement processes, thereby improving agency operations and overall CX. For example, AI can automate and streamline procurement operations, reducing paperwork, improving response times, and leading to faster procurement cycles. AI can also assist in supplier selection and product evaluation based on selective criteria such as quality, innovation, and sustainability. By leveraging AI algorithms to analyze supplier capabilities, track records, and product features, agencies can make informed decisions that align with customer expectations. This results in the procurement and delivery of high-quality products and services, enhancing overall CX for both internal users and suppliers.

On the strategic front, public procurement plays a crucial role in promoting responsible practices that contribute to CX and public value more broadly. AI can automate the evaluation process, enabling agencies to efficiently evaluate supplier sustainability performance, conduct environmental impact assessments, and assess the social and ethical aspects of suppliers' operations.[5] AI can also quickly analyze supplier databases and certifications to aid in identifying and evaluating a diverse range of suppliers, including local businesses, minority-owned enterprises, and social enterprises. This not only promotes inclusion through public procurement but also fosters economic development and social impact. Moreover, AI enhances transparency in the procurement process by monitoring and analyzing data across the supply chain and tracking suppliers' adherence to labor standards, environmental regulations, and ethical practices. Improved transparency helps identify potential risks and ensures that public procurement decisions align with broader public value.

This strategic use of AI in procurement can shape the overall CX by promoting a procurement process that is transparent, ethical, and integral, thereby increasing satisfaction among internal users, suppliers, citizens, and government officials.

Policy Obstacles: Design Principles for the Procurement of Ethical, Responsible, and Effective AI

Despite the clear benefits of AI in public procurement, extensive deployment in the public sector remains limited. This is largely due to policy issues that amplify the inherent challenges associated with AI, such as data security concerns, the complexity of decision-making processes, and the potential for bias and discrimination.[6] The absence of comprehensive policies guiding the design, procurement, and use of AI exacerbates these challenges, creating a barrier to the effective deployment of AI in public procurement.

In the face of these challenges, a policy framework can guide the procurement of AI technologies in a manner that fosters a positive CX, promotes ethical and responsible use of AI, and advances agency missions. To this end, seven design principles should be incorporated into such a policy framework. These principles aim to address the key challenges associated with AI and provide a roadmap for the responsible procurement and use of AI in the public sector. Table 1 at the end of this chapter summarizes their characteristics.

Principle 1: Adhere to Ethical Guidelines and Principles

AI technologies procured by public organizations should adhere to ethical guidelines and principles, which can promote responsible use, transparency, and accountability. Such AI tools, once deployed, can better contribute to a positive CX by ensuring that AI systems operate in a trustworthy and morally acceptable manner. For example, when procuring an AI-powered facial recognition system that may help to improve CX by streamlining identification verification processes, procurement agencies can ensure that systems adhere to ethical guidelines by incorporating fairness measures to mitigate biases and facilitating transparency through explainable algorithms.

Principle 2: Prioritize Privacy Protection

AI technologies procured by public organizations should prioritize privacy protection since doing so can help ensure that individuals' personal data are handled responsibly, protecting their personal data and privacy rights. This contributes to a positive CX by building trust and confidence in the organization's commitment to safeguarding personal information. For example, when procuring AI-driven data analytics platforms, procurement agencies can ensure tools have strong data anonymization and encryption protocols to protect individuals' personal information.

Principle 3. Address and Minimize Bias

AI technologies procured by public organizations should have protocols in place for addressing and minimizing the impacts of bias. Additionally, AI tools should have reliable methods for detecting potential biases and mechanisms in place to mitigate the harmful impacts of bias. By ensuring that AI systems do not discriminate or perpetuate systemic biases, organizations can promote fairness and equality in public service delivery.

For example, when procuring an AI-enabled recruitment system, procurement agencies can ensure that systems have undergone rigorous bias testing. Tools should also include features to identify and mitigate potential biases in the training data and algorithms to help avoid discriminatory outcomes and promote fairness in public sector hiring practices, enhancing the experience for job applicants.

Principle 4: Promote Interpretability and Explainability

AI technologies procured by public organizations should go beyond transparency to offer interpretability and explainability of AI-driven decisions. Interpretable and explainable AI can help empower customers by providing greater clarity about AI-driven decisions, increasing individuals' understanding of and trust in the decision.

For instance, when purchasing an AI-based system for processing applications for social assistance, procurement agencies can ensure that systems offer transparent explanations for the decisions they influence. This level of transparency can help individuals understand the factors that influenced whether their application was approved or denied, foster trust, and empower them to contest decisions, as is their right when they feel decisions may be biased or inaccurate.

Principle 5: Maximize Sustainability and Minimize Environmental Impact

AI technologies procured by public organizations should consider the sustainability and environmental impact of the AI technologies procured. Such actions can contribute uniquely to CX since sustainable AI systems can help to reduce waste and resource consumption, thereby promoting more efficient and economical organizations and more innovative and responsible means of delivering public services.

For example, when procuring an AI-driven waste management optimization system, procurement agencies can ensure that the system is designed to minimize fuel consumption and carbon emissions by optimizing routes and schedules. This can lead to more efficient service delivery with reduced environmental impact, often at a lower cost to taxpayers.

Principle 6: Promote Social Impact and Inclusion

AI technologies procured by public organizations should promote social impact and inclusion since government serves a diversity of needs, abilities, interests, and perspectives. Improving CX, especially for those who have been historically underserved, requires a level of awareness and sensitivity to the needs and experiences of those whom public organizations are meant to serve. AI tools, and especially the data that powers them, should best reflect the features, and needs of the public in order to enhance CX, as such tools can provide more accurate insights for designing services that are tailored, accessible, and inclusive of customers' needs.

For instance, when purchasing an AI-based language translation system for public schools, procurement agencies can ensure that it supports multiple languages and dialects, including those spoken by marginalized communities, to foster inclusivity and facilitate equal access to services.

Principle 7: Consider Responsible Vendor Governance

AI technologies procured by public organizations should be from vendors with responsible governance practices, as vendors with responsible governance practices can better ensure that AI solutions are designed with ethics, transparency, and accountability in mind. This contributes to CX by fostering trust in agencies and the services they deliver vis à vis the vendor's commitment to responsible AI use and delivery of high-quality products and services.

For example, procurement agencies should take responsible governance practices such as adherence to data privacy and security protocols into account when evaluating potential suppliers of AI technologies. Partnering with trustworthy vendors can, in turn, enhance customer trust and satisfaction and ensure the responsible development and use of AI.

LOOKING FORWARD

The responsible use of AI in the public sector is not only crucial for enhancing customer experience but also presents a unique opportunity for positive transformation of agency performance. However, realizing this potential requires addressing the challenges that AI poses, which demand strategies that go beyond currently established practices and perspectives.

The first step to take in addressing this challenge is acknowledging the complexity of the full-service delivery experience, including the systems, people, and processes that contribute to a great CX. This includes recognizing the critical and unique role that public procurement plays in the deployment and use of AI.

Public procurement is instrumental in two key ways. First, procurement processes are responsible for the acquisition of ethical, responsible, and trustworthy AI technologies that can enhance CX by improving customer satisfaction and public trust. Second, the use of AI to streamline and improve procurement processes can have downstream effects that contribute to the overall CX. However, the potential of AI in public procurement remains largely untapped due to policy issues that amplify the inherent challenges associated with AI.

To address these issues, the seven design principles described in this chapter can guide the evaluation and procurement of AI technologies. These principles aim to foster a positive CX while promoting the ethical and responsible use of AI in the public sector. These principles are not meant to be exhaustive nor definitive but rather to serve as a starting point for the development of comprehensive AI policies in the public sector. They provide a framework for assessing, evaluating, and procuring AI technologies, with a focus on promoting ethical, responsible, and customer-centric AI tools and their deployment.

The principles also prompt further empirical exploration to understand their strengths, weaknesses, and impacts on AI deployments in the public sector for CX. While there are numerous examples of successful AI integration in public organizations, there have also been numerous failed attempts. These efforts provide fertile ground for the development of case studies to better understand why the implementation of new technology policy tools is sometimes unsuccessful. As such, they should be the focus of researchers and practitioners alike.

In conclusion, the ideas put forth in this chapter, particularly the seven design principles serve as a compass for agencies to navigate the complexities of AI adoption. They provide a roadmap for maximizing the benefits of AI, paving the way toward a future where responsible AI tools can help agencies deliver a great experience for customers, thereby building public trust and enhancing the relationship between government and the people it serves.

Table 1. Design Principles for Ethical Use of AI in and through Public Procurement

Principle	Meaning	Impact on CX	Implementation Tools
1. Ethical Guidelines and Principles	Procure AI technologies that adhere to ethical standards and guidelines	Builds trust and confidence in AI systems, ensuring ethical and accountable use	Vendor assessments, ethical guidelines framework, code of conduct for vendors
2. Privacy Protection	Prioritize privacy protection in AI technologies and data handling	Enhances customer trust and confidence in the protection of personal information	Privacy impact assessments, data anonymization techniques, encryption protocols
3. Bias Minimization	Minimize and address biases in AI technologies to ensure fairness and equality	Provides inclusive and unbiased services, enhancing customer trust and satisfaction	Bias testing and mitigation frameworks, fairness metrics, diverse training data sets
4. Interpretability and Explainability	Procure AI technologies that are interpretable and explainable	Enhances transparency and clarity in AI decision-making, increasing customer trust	Explainable AI algorithms, model interpretability techniques, decision-making documentation
5. Sustainability and Environmental Impact	Consider sustainability and minimize environmental impact in AI technologies	Optimizes resource consumption, reduces waste, and promotes energy efficiency	Sustainable procurement criteria, carbon footprint assessment, energy-efficient AI models
6. Social Impact and Inclusion	Promote social impact and inclusion in AI technologies	Provides tailored, accessible, and inclusive services, enhancing customer experience	Accessibility standards, diverse data sets, inclusion, and diversity criteria in procurement
7. Responsible Vendor Governance	Procure AI technologies from vendors with responsible governance practices	Fosters trust in vendors' commitment to responsible AI use, ensuring quality products and services	Vendor assessments, governance frameworks, compliance requirements, contractual obligations

Ana-Maria Dimand, *PhD, is Assistant Professor of Public Policy and Admin-istration School of Public Service at Boise State University. Her research focuses on public management, specifically on issues related to government contracting, collaborative governance, innovation and sustainability.*

Kayla Schwoerer, *PhD, is an Assistant Professor in the Department of Public Administration & Policy at Rockefeller College (University at Albany, SUNY) and an Assistant Professor in the Department of Public Adminis-tration and Political Science at Vrije Universiteit (VU) in Amsterdam. Her research focuses broadly on the intersection of public and nonprofit man-agement, science, technology and innovation studies, and social equity.*

Andrea S. Patrucco, *PhD, is an Assistant Professor of Supply Chain Man-agement Department of Marketing and Logistics at the College of Business, Florida International University, in Miami, Florida. His research interests are in the field of management of buyer-supplier relationships in both the pri-vate and public sectors.*

Ilia Murtazashvili, *PhD, is Professor of Public Policy and Political Economy and Co-Director of the Center for Governance and Markets at the University of Pittsburgh and a Research Partner with SpectrumX: An NSF Spectrum Innovation Center. At the Center for Governance and Markets, Ilia leads the Research Program on Governance of Emerging Technologies.*

Endnotes

1   Hickok, Merve. "Public procurement of artificial intelligence systems: new risks and future proofing." AI & society (2022): 1-15. https://doi.org/10.1007/s00146-022-01572-2 World Economic Forum. "Unlocking Public Sector Artificial Intelligence."

2   World Economic Forum. "Unlocking Public Sector Artificial Intelligence." https://www.weforum.org/projects/unlocking-public-sector-artificial-intelligence.

3   Dor, Lavi M. Ben, and Cary Coglianese. "Procurement as AI governance." *IEEE Transac-tions on Technology and Society* 2, no. 4 (2021): 192-199.

4   Chenok, Dan. "How Can Governments Use AI to Improve Procurement?" *The Regulatory Review*, June 30, 2022, https://www.theregreview.org/2022/06/30/chenok-how-can-governments-use-ai-to-improve-procurement/.

5   Ahmadi, Mohammad and Dr. Justin B. Bullock, *Government Procurement and Acquisi-tion: Opportunities and Challenges Presented by Artificial Intelligence and Machine Learn-ing*, IBM Center for The Business of Government, Washington, D.C., 2023.

6   Autio, Chloe, Kate Cummings, Brinson S. Elliot, and Beth Simone Noveck. "A Snapshot of Artificial Intelligence Procurement Challenges: Diagnosing perceived and actual risks impeding responsible AI acquisitions in government." June 2023. The GovLab. https://files.thegovlab.org/a-snapshot-of-ai-procurement-challenges-june2023.pdf.

Chapter Nine

Quantum Technology Challenge: What Role for the Government?

By Paula Ganga
Stanford University

INTRODUCTION

Quantum technology has the potential to reshape the economic and social landscape of the world. The U.S. has already invested significant resources in developing quantum information science (QIS), but more needs to be done as government operations could bear the brunt of the disruptions and possible attacks.

As the U.S. invests the resources to develop this technology and maintain a strategic lead over other countries, cybersecurity—as one of the earliest sectors impacted—will be at the forefront of future developments. Yet the government should not overlook the environmental and sustainability issues that quantum technology entails or the training of a skilled workforce that can proficiently use these technological advances.

This chapter first discusses what quantum technology is and how it could change government functioning. Next, the chapter examines the impact on cybersecurity and cryptography, as well as how quantum might impact environmental sustainability and labor. The last sections of the chapter focus on effective policymaking to make the best use of this emerging technology.

What is Quantum Computing?

Quantum computing makes use of quantum phenomena such as superposition and entanglement to perform faster computations.[1] Quantum physics differs from classical physics in a variety of ways. At the most basic level, understanding quantum starts by distinguishing between the basic unit of analysis in each of these two conceptions of the world.

In classical physics—and the computers based on it—information is stored in binary bits that can take the values of zero or one. In quantum physics, quantum bits (or qubits) can represent both zero and one (or a combination of the two) at the same time. This phenomenon of superposition allows quantum computers to find faster solutions to mathematical problems that currently take classical computers significantly more time and computing capacity.[2]

Comparing complex computational tasks to finding the way out of a maze, a classical computer tries to solve the maze by following every path in sequence until reaching the exit, but superposition allows a quantum computer to try all the paths at once.[3] This drastically reduces the time to find a solution. Increasing the number of qubits results in a dramatic increase in the calculation processing speed.[4] Additionally, various quantum algorithms offer substantial speedups relative to classical algorithms. For example, Gover's and Shor's algorithms each promise a polynomial and an exponential speedup[5] respectively over a classical computer.[6]

The real-world applications of this computational breakthrough can be revolutionizing. In a May 2022 White House National Memorandum, the Biden administration acknowledged the importance of quantum computing for fields as diverse as materials science, pharmaceuticals, finance, and energy.[7] However, that same memorandum sounded the alarm bells for the risks posed by vulnerabilities in existing systems once quantum technology was fully developed. Despite its still mostly theoretical nature, breakthroughs in quantum technology have happened at an accelerated pace in recent years, dramatically hastening the timeline to a fully functioning quantum computer being only 5 to 10 years away.[8]

Preparing for the Future

In the same memorandum, the Biden administration stated that "while the full range of applications of quantum computers is still unknown, it is nevertheless clear that America's continued technological and scientific leadership will depend, at least in part, on the nation's ability to maintain a competitive advantage in quantum computing and QIS."[9] To this end, the U.S. government has already started to invest substantial efforts and resources in quantum information technology.

By the numbers
In fiscal year (FY) 2022, the U.S. budget for research and development in quantum computing reached about $900 million, which is double the amount spent in 2019. For example, in the case of the U.S. Department of Defense (DOD), budget requests focusing on quantum-related programs increased by 37 percent between FY2020 and FY2022.[10] According to a report by the National Science and Technology Council Subcommittee on Quantum Information Science, much of this increase in spending was done for activities related to the National Quantum Initiative (NQI) Act, signed into law in 2018.[11]

In FY2023, the U.S. Department of Energy (DOE) received a total of $245 million, including $125 million for five of the DOE-led National QIS Research Centers.[12] The National Institutes of Health's Office of Data Science received $85 million, in order to implement a new pilot program with the DOE to study the role of quantum computing in biomedical sciences.[13] The National Science Foundation (NSF) received $235 million to continue QIS R&D, including $50 million for research at NQIS Research Centers. The National Institute of Standards and Technology (NIST) funding for QIS reached $54 million.[14] DOD saw several program increases such as $30 million for USAF

Ion Trap Quantum Computing, $10 million for USAF Quantum Network
Testbed, $5 million for USAF Secure Quantum Computing Facility, $30 million for university-based quantum materials applied research, $10 million
for Army quantum technologies for armament systems, and $1.4 million for
quantum computing technologies.[15]

Agility versus redundancy
The recent growth in QIS R&D is driven in part by NQI activities. Among
these activities is the establishment of institutions such as quantum consortia by NIST, Quantum Leap Challenge Institutes through NSF, and National
Quantum Information Science Research Centers by the DOE.[16]

This flurry of research centers, consortia, and institutes across multiple agencies could be confusing. While this activity is meant to create sufficient
opportunities for work on quantum technologies to be developed as widely as
possible, it may also create redundancies and function overlap. Congress, in
acts mentioning quantum, recognizes the need for urgency in quantum development, but the extent to which government reaches the desired levels of agility and flexibility in developing this technology will depend on how efficiently
and effectively these funds reach their target. Moreover, combining government
action with initiatives from private actors could create a multiplier effect, but it
could also have public and private actors work at cross purposes.

Cybersecurity and the Cryptography Competition

The May 2022 White House Memorandum stressed that quantum computing and QIS can create critical challenges in data protection: "A quantum
computer of sufficient size and sophistication—also known as a cryptanalytically relevant quantum computer (CRQC)—will be capable of breaking much
of the public-key cryptography used on digital systems across the U.S. and
around the world. When it becomes available, a CRQC could jeopardize civilian and military communications, undermine supervisory and control systems
for critical infrastructure, and defeat security protocols for most internet-based
financial transactions."[17] The computing power of this new technology in the
hands of malicious actors could cripple the functioning of the government and
the economy. Critical data and infrastructure in the U.S. have been targeted by
hackers for years.[18] Access to quantum computing could exacerbate this trend
if the government cannot quantum-proof its encryption algorithms.[19]

Competition on multiple levels
At this point, even today's most advanced classical computers and cryptanalysis techniques cannot easily break current types of encryption. However, a fully
functioning quantum computer could break an asymmetric key algorithm in a

matter of minutes.[20] Successful attacks against these algorithms could compromise the financial system, critical infrastructure, and military installations.[21]

The dangers of quantum decryption are not only coming from individuals or hacker collectives but also other governments. Much has been written about China having possibly outpaced the U.S. in various applications such as quantum networks and quantum processors.[22] Additionally, the National Counterintelligence and Security Center identifies quantum computing—along with AI, bioeconomy, autonomous systems, and semiconductors—as one of the strategic technology sectors where the U.S. faces growing challenges from China and an increasingly long list of countries.[23] Although these five technologies have been singled out as particularly challenging by the U.S. government, experts argue that combining them could be even more dangerous. For example, Quantum Artificial Intelligence—a combination of quantum technology and AI—could compound the disruptive capacity of both technologies.[24] Any information assumed secure today could be captured and stored to be deciphered later once sufficiently powerful quantum computers are created. Hackers or hostile governments could seize currently encrypted personal or financial data and decipher it retroactively.[25]

Sustainable Quantum

The importance of QIS to fight climate change is one of the most significant advantages experts and government officials mention when justifying continued investment in this technology. The increased computational power of quantum computing can help with tasks as complex as developing new sustainable materials or new sources of renewable energy by:

- Running simulations to test the energy production and efficiency of new materials

- Creating more efficient batteries and cheaper quantum-enabled solar panels

- Improving agriculture and $CO2$ emissions by streamlining the production of ammonia for agricultural use

- Ramping up carbon capture and carbon sequestration activity

- Improving delivery routes and transportation inefficiencies

- Finding favorable locations for wind and solar farms so they can harvest the greatest amount of natural energy[26]

These possible benefits compound the already higher computational efficiency predicted for quantum computers compared to classical computers.

According to studies conducted by NASA, Google, and the Oak Ridge National Laboratory, a quantum computer might only require 0.002 percent of the energy consumed by a classical supercomputer to perform the same task with a peak power rating of 25kW.[27] Compared with current supercomputers which sometimes need as much electricity as a small town, a functioning quantum computer can solve problems in a few hours with much less energy.

Challenges to sustainable physical quantum hardware: cooling and noise

Currently, the biggest energy consumption of quantum computers comes from the need to keep chips extremely cold in order to perform. The slightest temperature fluctuation can mean that atoms and molecules move around too much, potentially causing a qubit to inadvertently change its quantum state. To this end, temperatures in some parts of the quantum circuit can be 250 times colder than deep space.[28] In addressing this problem, IBM built a super-fridge named Goldeneye to house its largest quantum computers and conduct future experiments. Goldeneye, despite its large size, requires less space than other large-scale dilution refrigerators to house the same amount of hardware.[29] While efficiency gains are important in developing these larger cooling facilities, the cost of building and operating them is still extremely high considering the future expansion of this technology.

Temperature fluctuations are not the only environmental conditions that can impact quantum computers' functioning. Environmental "noise" can destroy the fragile quantum state of qubits and lead to dephasing. For the longest time, researchers had developed statistics-based models to estimate the impact of unwanted "Gaussian noise" surrounding qubits,[30] but new methods have been developed to deal with non-Gaussian noise and protect qubits from specific noise types.[31]

Many of these solutions have focused on modeling noise[32] such as the "bosonic dephasing channel" model.[33] Both noise and temperature issues show the difficulty in building physical quantum hardware that performs well enough to produce the expected results. Investment in these machines is substantial and much work needs to be done in order to deal with the temperature and noise requirements for a highly sensitive, highly performing quantum computer. In the context of these and other factors that lead to decoherence of the quantum state, a sustainable quantum computing program needs to directly take on these challenges to deliver on the promise of a fully functioning quantum computer in the next 5 to 10 years.[34]

The future is hybrid

To avoid these pitfalls, a host of solutions have been devised. To deal with the exacting requirements for extreme cooling in quantum computing, new initiatives have spurred the development of room-temperature quantum computers.[35] The world's first room-temperature quantum computer was developed in Germany and is housed at a supercomputing facility in Australia. While the synthetic diamond chip of this computer can only handle 5 qubits compared to over 400 qubits in some of the more advanced quantum computers, because it does not require any cooling infrastructure it can work alongside classical computers and can be more easily integrated into existing systems. This approach is cheaper to build, own, and run, thus bringing quantum technology closer to end users.[36]

In addressing noise, current approaches have focused on modeling the type and source of noise—but considering that this issue also tries to address the impact of environmental conditions on the quantum state of the qubit, a similar hybrid approach should be considered. A hybrid model is one in which the classical computing platform is sitting at one end of the system, and the qubits in the quantum computer at the other. Bridging the two are control processors making hybridization possible, one operating at room temperature to link with the classical computer and one at cryogenic temperatures to monitor the qubits. The two parts of the system divide tasks with the quantum computer handling the hard problems, while the classical systems perform routine tasks.[37] Today many of the quantum systems, from IonQ to D-Wave to Rigetti, are hybrid.

As the U.S. government continues to prioritize both environmental sustainability and quantum technology, investing in hybrid quantum computers should become an important part of the agenda.

The Quantum Workforce

Because quantum computing functions on a completely different paradigm from classical computing both for hardware and software, an important challenge is the expertise required to create working products that leverage this innovation. Right now, only a small very highly skilled elite workforce has the knowledge required to work in this field. In 2021 there was only one qualified candidate for every three quantum jobs available,[38] and the gap continues to persist.[39]

This means that only a small elite workforce has the skills to contribute to these developments and fill jobs in this field. To overcome workforce limitations and democratize access to these powerful systems, many suggest investing more in basic STEM knowledge as early as possible,[40] while another approach has been to develop ready-to-run quantum software that subject matter experts with no quantum experience can use in hybrid classical-quantum computing systems.[41]

Overcoming the talent gap
Through the National Quantum Initiative Act of 2018, the U.S. has already allocated funding for the development of a quantum workforce. Among the points of this action plan are objectives such as:

- Encouraging the creation of collaborations between industry and academic institutions

- Using and improving existing programs to increase the quantum workforce

- Encouraging academic institutions to consider quantum science and engineering as a different discipline in need of new teachers, curricula, and initiatives

- Starting quantum science education as early as primary schools

- Targeting the wider public so that quantum science knowledge increases at the level of the whole society[42]

The great educational requirements for this overhaul of the American workforce explain the high number of quantum-focused institutions recommended by the U.S. government and funded through the NQI.

LOOKING FORWARD

Recommendations for Leveraging Quantum Computing

For the government to fully benefit from the advances of quantum computing, early investment has been crucial as shown by the resources allocated so far. But the roles the government can play in QIS are multifaceted. To make the best of this investment, several roles and policy recommendations stand out alongside existing government policy.

A leader in cybersecurity

In the case of cybersecurity, a two-pronged approach is required. This means not just investment in quantum technology but also in better classical encryption. Right now, hackers routinely exploit vulnerabilities in network encryption and download sensitive data, which could be decrypted later when quantum decryption catches up. With the data already downloaded, accessing this sensitive information will not be hard. Thus, the government needs to switch from being the object of cyberattacks to proactively addressing cybersecurity in both classical and quantum terms. This proposal requires collaboration across a multitude of actors both domestic and international to prevent bad-faith actors from attacking the system—whether hackers or other governments. The U.S. has already hosted an international roundtable in May 2022 with the heads of quantum strategy offices in Australia, Canada, Denmark, Finland, France, Germany, Japan, the Netherlands, Sweden, Switzerland, and the UK.[43] The next step would be to expand this cooperation and create more permanent systems for collaboration.

Supporter of industry initiatives

In the case of quantum sustainability, another two-front approach is recommended. The U.S. government should pursue both increasing efficiency for cooling technology and "noise" reduction in quantum computing, but also developing hybrid quantum computers. This will allow the U.S. to continue housing quantum computers with the largest number of qubits, but also develop smaller hybrid quantum computers for easier integration in the wider economy. Only continued development in both technologies can ensure U.S. "quantum supremacy."

Quantum innovator

Finally, in the field of quantum education and training, the U.S. government can become an innovator by adding to existing educational initiatives and research centers, taking a new hands-on approach to quantum training on the job. As quantum technology becomes more available and more employees use it, the U.S. government should not rely only on students currently in STEM training. This could leave millions of U.S. workers out of the economic benefits of the quantum revolution. The government instead can take the lead by creating pilot programs to train employees in its own ranks. As the nation's largest employer, the government can leverage this position to start creating the quantum workforce of the future from within, and expand the training developed through this educational initiative as widely as possible throughout the U.S. economy.

Current debates about whether AI may lead to eliminating jobs show the importance of dealing with the impact of technological progress as soon as possible. To avoid the economic dislocations and inequalities that may accompany a new technology—whether steam power, AI, or quantum—the government can play an active role not only in mitigating the difficult economic consequences, but in shepherding innovation via policy.

Paula Ganga, PhD, is an Assistant Professor of Political Economy at Duke Kunshan University and a Visiting Fellow at Stanford University. She was a Postdoctoral Fellow at Columbia University's Harriman Institute and the Skalny Center for Polish and Central European Studies at the University of Rochester after completing her doctorate at Georgetown University.

Endnotes

1   For a basic introduction to quantum computing see LaPierre, Ray, *Introduction to quantum computing* (Springer Nature, 2021) https://link.springer.com/book/10.1007/978-3-030-69318-3.

2   World Economic Forum, *State of Quantum Computing: Building a Quantum Economy*, September 2022, pp. 5-6, https://www.weforum.org/reports/state-of-quantum-computing-building-a-quantum-economy/.

3   Campbell, Charlie, "Quantum Computers Could Solve Countless Problems—And Create a Lot of New Ones," *Time*, January 26, 2023, https://time.com/6249784/quantum-computing-revolution/.

4   In an example provided by Deodoro et al., "two traditional binary bits are needed to match the power of a single qubit; four bits are required to match two qubits; eight bits are needed to match three qubits; and so on. It would take about 18 quadrillion bits of traditional memory to model a quantum computer with just 54 qubits. A 100-qubit quantum computer would require more bits than there are atoms on our planet. And a 280-qubit computer would require more bits than there are atoms in the known universe." (Deodoro, Jose, Michael Gorbanyov, Majid Malaika and Tahsin Saadi Sedik, "Quantum Computing and the Financial System: Spooky Action at a Distance?" (*IMF Working Papers*, 2021), 6.)

5   A polynomial speedup is when a quantum computer can solve a problem in time T, compared to a classical computer which would need the longer time T^2. In the case of an exponential speedup, the classical computer needs time 2^T.

6   Deodoro et al., "Quantum," 6.

7   The White House, "National Security Memorandum on Promoting United States Leadership in Quantum Computing While Mitigating Risks to Vulnerable Cryptographic Systems," May 4, 2022, https://www.whitehouse.gov/briefing-room/statements-releases/2022/05/04/national-security-memorandum-on-promoting-united-states-leadership-in-quantum-computing-while-mitigating-risks-to-vulnerable-cryptographic-systems/.

8   Kelley, Alexandra, "The White House announced new plans to promote quantum technology research and development while helping U.S. computer networks transition to post-quantum cryptography standards," May 4, 2022, https://www.nextgov.com/emerging-tech/2022/05/white-house-issues-two-quantum-directives-set-bolster-american-infrastructure/366483/.

9   White House, "National Security Memorandum."

10 Gross, Natalie, "Where Is Quantum Technology Going in the Federal Government?," *FedTech Magazine*, June 29, 2022, https://fedtechmagazine.com/article/2022/06/where-quantum-technology-going-federal-government.

11   National Science and Technology Council, "National Quantum Initiative. Supplement to the President's FY 2022 Budget," December 2021, https://www.quantum.gov/wp-content/uploads/2021/12/NQI-Annual-Report-FY2022.pdf.

12   Villano, Peter, "More Money, More Guidance for Quantum Information Science R&D," Federal Budget IQ, January 27, 2023, https://federalbudgetiq.com/insights/more-money-more-guidance-for-quantum-information-science-rd/.

13   U.S. Senate, "Congressional Record. PROCEEDINGS AND DEBATES OF THE 117th CONGRESS, SECOND SESSION," December 20, 2022, S8553, Vol. 168 , No. 198—Book II, p. S8885, https://www.congress.gov/117/crec/2022/12/20/168/198/CREC-2022-12-20-pt2-PgS8553-2.pdf.

14   U.S. Congress, "DIVISION B—COMMERCE, JUSTICE, SCIENCE, AND RELATED AGENCIES APPROPRIATIONS ACT, 2023," p. 11-12, https://www.appropriations.senate.gov/imo/media/doc/Division%20B%20-%20CJS%20Statement%20FY23.pdf.

15   U.S. Congress, "DIVISION C - DEPARTMENT OF DEFENSE APPROPRIATIONS ACT, 2023," p. 89A, p. 94B, https://www.appropriations.senate.gov/imo/media/doc/Division%20C%20-%20Defense%20Statement%20FY23.pdf.

16   Gross, "Where"; Villano, "More."

17   White House, "National Security Memorandum."

18   Department of Justice (DOJ), "U.S. Department of Justice Disrupts Hive Ransomware Variant," January 26, 2023, https://www.justice.gov/opa/pr/us-department-justice-disrupts-hive-ransomware-variant.

19   "NIST Announces First Four Quantum-Resistant Cryptographic Algorithms," July 05, 2022, https://www.nist.gov/news-events/news/2022/07/nist-announces-first-four-quantum-resistant-cryptographic-algorithms.

20   Pflitsch, Markus, "Quantum Computers Could Make Today's Encryption Defenseless," Forbes, May 3, 2023, https://www.forbes.com/sites/forbestechcouncil/2023/05/04/quantum-computers-could-make-todays-encryption-defenseless/?sh=207bd31d8556.

21   Sedik, Tahsin Saadi, Majid Malaika, Michael Gorbanyov, and Jose Deodoro, "Quantum Computing's Possibilities and Perils," International Monetary Fund, September 2021, https://www.imf.org/en/Publications/fandd/issues/2021/09/quantum-computings-possibilitiesand-perils-deodoro.

22   Corbett, Thomas and Peter W. Singer, "China May Have Just Taken the Lead in the Quantum Computing Race," Defense One, April 14, 2022, https://www.defenseone.com/ideas/2022/04/china-may-have-just-taken-lead-quantum-computing-race/365707/; Wadhwa, Vivek and Mauritz Kop, "Why Quantum Computing Is Even More Dangerous Than Artificial Intelligence," Foreign Policy, August 21, 2022, https://foreignpolicy.com/2022/08/21/quantum-computing-artificial-intelligence-ai-technology-regulation/.

23   National Counterintelligence and Security Center, "Protecting Critical and Emerging US Technologies from Foreign Threats," October 2021, https://www.dni.gov/files/NCSC/documents/SafeguardingOurFuture/FINAL _ NCSC _ Emerging%20Technologies _ Factsheet _ 10 _ 22 _ 2021.pdf.

24   Taylor, Richard D., "Quantum artificial intelligence: a "Precautionary" U.S. approach?" Telecommunications Policy 44, no. 6 (2020): 101909.

25   Campbell, Charlie, "Quantum Computers Could Solve Countless Problems—And Create a Lot of New Ones," Time, January 26, 2023, https://time.com/6249784/quantum-computing-revolution/.

26   Cooper, Peter, Philipp Ernst, Dieter Kiewell, and Dickon Pinner, "Quantum computing just might save the planet," McKinsey Digital, May 19, 2022, https://www.mckinsey.com/capabilities/mckinsey-digital/our-insights/quantum-computing-just-might-save-the-planet; Pflitsch, Markus, "Will Quantum Technology Be The Silver Bullet For Climate Change?," Forbes, September 2, 2022, https://www.forbes.com/sites/forbestechcouncil/2022/09/02/will-quantum-technology-be-the-silver-bullet-for-climate-change/?sh=34272e783c1f.

27   Wu, Tin Lok, "What is Quantum Computing and How Can it Help Mitigate Climate Change?" Earth.Org, August 22, 2022, https://earth.org/what-is-quantum-computing/#:~:text=In%20addition%20to%20its%20functions,to%20perform%20the%20same%20task; Wogan, Tim, "Quantum computers vastly outperform supercomputers when it comes to energy efficiency," *Physics World*, May 01, 2020, https://physicsworld.com/a/quantum-computers-vastly-outperform-supercomputers-when-it-comes-to-energy-efficiency/.

28   Moss, Sebastian, "Cooling quantum computers," January 27, 2021, https://www.datacenterdynamics.com/en/analysis/cooling-quantum-computers/.

29   Lapienyté, Jurgita, "IBM builds super-fridge for quantum computers," *Cyber News*, September 08, 2022, https://cybernews.com/tech/ibm-builds-super-fridge-for-quantum-computers/.

30   Gaussian noise can be compared to white noise coming from the murmuring of a large crowd, whereas non-Gaussian noise features distinctive patterns from a few particularly strong noise sources. See Rob Matheson, "Uncovering the hidden "noise" that can kill qubits," September 16, 2019, https://news.mit.edu/2019/non-gaussian-noise-detect-qubits-0916.

31   Sung, Youngkyu, Félix Beaudoin, Leigh M. Norris, Fei Yan, David K. Kim, Jack Y. Qiu, Uwe von Lüpke, Jonilyn L. Yoder, Terry P. Orlando, Simon Gustavsson, Lorenza Viola and William D. Oliver, "Non-Gaussian noise spectroscopy with a superconducting qubit sensor," *Nature Communications* 10, 3715 (2019). https://doi.org/10.1038/s41467-019-11699-4.

32   Katwala, Amit, "Quantum Computing Has a Noise Problem," January 17, 2023, https://www.wired.com/story/fixing-quantum-computing-noise-algorithmiq/.

33   Lami, Ludovico and Mark M. Wilde, "Exact solution for the quantum and private capacities of bosonic dephasing channels," *Nature Photonics*, 2023, DOI: 10.1038/s41566-023-01190-4; *Science Daily*, "How to overcome noise in quantum computations," April 6, 2023, https://www.sciencedaily.com/releases/2023/04/230406113922.htm.

34   Kelley, "The White House."

35   Skyrme, Tess, "The Status of Room-Temperature Quantum Computers," March 20, 2023, https://www.eetimes.eu/the-status-of-room-temperature-quantum-computers/.

36   Flaherty, Nick, "First room-temperature quantum computer in supercomputing centre," June 2, 2022, https://www.eenewseurope.com/en/first-room-temperature-quantum-computer-in-supercomputing-centre/; Midgley, Stuart, "The world's first room-temperature quantum computer brings the future a step closer, " March 26, 2021, https://dug.com/the-worlds-first-room-temperature-quantum-computer-brings-the-future-a-step-closer/.

37   Herman, Arthur, "The Quantum Revolution Is Here, Its Name Is Hybrid," April 29, 2022, https://www.forbes.com/sites/arthurherman/2022/04/29/the-quantum-revolution-is-here-its-name-is-hybrid/?sh=29b6c71540fa.

38   Masiowski, Mateusz, Niko Mohr, Henning Soller, and Matija Zesko, "Quantum computing funding remains strong, but talent gap raises concern," *McKinsey Digital*, June 15, 2022, https://www.mckinsey.com/capabilities/mckinsey-digital/our-insights/quantum-computing-funding-remains-strong-but-talent-gap-raises-concern#/.

39   Mohr, Niko, Kiera Peltz, Rodney Zemmel, and Matija Zesko, "Five lessons from AI on closing quantum's talent gap—before it's too late," *McKinsey Digital*, December 1, 2022, https://www.mckinsey.com/capabilities/mckinsey-digital/our-insights/five-lessons-from-ai-on-closing-quantums-talent-gap-before-its-too-late.

40   Peterssen, Guido, "Quantum Technology Impact: The Necessary Workforce for Developing Quantum Software," in QANSWER, 2020, pp. 6-22.

41   van Velzen, Julian, "The Future Of Quantum Computing Requires An Emerging Quantum Workforce," *Forbes*, March 1, 2023, https://www.forbes.com/sites/forbestechcouncil/2023/03/01/the-future-of-quantum-computing-requires-an-emerging-quantum-workforce/?sh=5037145c4239.

42   Peterssen, "Quantum," 14.

43   *Quantum.gov*, "International Roundtable on Pursuing Quantum Information Together: 2^N vs 2N," May 9, 2022, https://www.quantum.gov/readout-international-roundtable-2n/.

Chapter Ten

Using Linked Administrative Data to Advance Evidence-Based Policymaking

By Stephanie Walsh and Kevin Dehmer
Rutgers University

INTRODUCTION

Government agencies are rich with administrative data related to who they serve and how they serve them, but the infrastructure is typically purpose-built for the specific needs of the agency. Despite these robust data sources, they are rarely central to decision-making processes because of data limitations and staff training or capacity.

A central constraint on a broader use of administrative data to inform policy is its siloed nature. Take, for example, a state Department of Education that maintains thousands of data points on the administration of its services and students served. While this department can produce the necessary metrics to understand what is happening to students in K-12 within the confines of their services, it would lack the ability to connect that information with data from supplemental sources. This inhibits the ability to learn more about what students experience outside of school, and beyond their K-12 education, to understand the impacts of the curricula and supports delivered during a student's time in school.

This chapter explores how to improve the use of existing administrative data based on a case study of a Statewide Longitudinal Data System (SLDS). SLDS can break down silos within government, facilitate shared governance, and answer research questions between state partners, while highlighting the benefits of data driven decision making. The use of SLDS data is transforming evidence-based policymaking, providing a model for how states and other governmental entities can better leverage administrative data for a broader set of purposes.

The use of SLDS data, leveraging advances in artificial intelligence and streamlined data governance, is transforming evidence-based policymaking, making each agency's existing data more powerful when connected to partners. Continued enhancements to the SLDS provide a model for how states and other governmental entities can better leverage administrative data for a broader set of purposes.

Leveraging the Increasing Availability of Administrative Data

The availability of administrative data in some countries has facilitated an abundance of important research that tracks public performance and improves service delivery. Some Nordic countries, such as Denmark, Sweden, Norway, and Finland, are decades into the development and use of their administrative data following the introduction of population-wide identifiers.[1]

For example, in 2005, linked family and individual longitudinal administrative data allowed researchers in Denmark to conduct a study on the effects of parental education on their children's education.[2] Similar studies expand these types of analyses to health and labor market outcomes. Understanding such causal effects allows policymakers to target resources more efficiently and adjust implementation, while monitoring to ensure that public programs are working as intended.

Historically, there have been fewer such partnerships and data use in the United States—but the need remains.

Current Status and Opportunities of Statewide Longitudinal Data Systems

Linked administrative data, considered infeasible even just a decade ago, represents an enormous leap forward to policymakers who seek to demonstrate and maximize the effectiveness of public resources. For instance, a higher education agency collects data on postsecondary participation and outcomes. The agency can assess the effectiveness of certain financial aid or academic support programs on performance, retention, and completion of a postsecondary degree. However, many factors impact those outcomes beyond what is collected at institutions of higher education, such as details from K-12 education, participation in the labor force, food insecurity, or health concerns. Better access and use of those important features of a student's life, using longitudinal data already collected across multiple agencies, can help leaders make more informed and holistic policy to support their stakeholders.

The current Statewide Longitudinal Data Systems, administered by the U.S. Department of Education's (ED) National Center for Education Statistics, includes a guiding principle of the SLDS grant program that "better decisions require better information." Since the first round of grants in 2005, nearly all U.S. states and territories have received an SLDS grant from ED to develop, expand, or use linked administrative data. With this support, states have made significant progress from siloed agency data developing collaborative interagency partnerships and data sharing to build evidence-based policy.

New Jersey, for instance, received its first SLDS grant in 2012 to support the foundational work of legal agreements, governing practices, data sharing, and infrastructure. The state's second grant in 2019 enabled building on that progress to update infrastructure and interoperability, as well as piloting initiatives for external data access. The state seeks to further its SLDS mission of enabling longitudinal data to improve governance efforts, policymaking, and the performance of public initiatives. The development of New Jersey's SLDS has allowed the state to replace previous manual data collection efforts on student financial aid program outcomes with an automated annual report that relies on cross-departmental data. Similarly, the state recently passed legislation requiring the use of the SLDS to develop an annual teacher workforce report, producing regular updates on potential shortages and nuanced trends that can inform policy strategies through the use of linked administrative data.

Continuing the example of a state's Department of Education, the SLDS system affords the opportunity to build on what the state knows about their students in the classroom and adds details about whether they are working while completing high school, in a household experiencing poverty, or at-risk of homelessness. Critically, these systems further allow for examination of what happens to their students after they leave high school—whether they attend postsecondary education or attend a vocational training program and, ultimately, their employment experiences.

Having this type of information and evidence strengthens service delivery in two primary ways. First, they can identify students who might be at risk of not completing high school earlier and connect them and their family with the supports they need. Second, they can use evidence of past student experience to determine the types of curricula, support, and programming that have the biggest impacts. For instance, data about remedial coursework in postsecondary can help secondary programs change approaches to improve preparedness for college or other training programs, and suggest which state programs had the biggest impact on student postsecondary to career success. Such data-based questions have typically not been addressed in a formal way, but by using SLDS systems, these questions can be both answered and routinely monitored to provide regular feedback to policymakers.

With a well-functioning SLDS, agencies can no longer operate in silos. They can lean on the infrastructure developed by ED, expand with similar grants from the U.S. Department of Labor, and prioritize state funding to get the information they need to best serve their constituents. Experience with these systems has demonstrated that this value is not limited to K-12 education, but expands into all public administration. Programs operate better, more efficiently, and more effectively when provided with real evidence on policy outcomes. Over time, these and similar investments in shared data systems could well pay for themselves by making public programs more efficient and effective.

Transforming Evidence-Based Policymaking Through Linked Data

The use of SLDS data, combined with the leveraging of advances in computing technology and streamlined data governance, is transforming evidence-based policymaking in multiple ways:

Facilitates shared governance. The development and use of an SLDS also facilitates shared governance by creating a forum for agencies to work together toward research questions that are a priority across agencies. This helps to build trust and strengthens partnerships among agencies, and ensures that data are used in an accurate, consistent, and ethical way with shared governance and input from the data owners in all data use. Ultimately, this type of collaboration leads to better decision making—all stakeholders at the table allows policy to be informed by a wider range of data and experts to better serve the public.

Enables real-time data analysis and streamlined reporting. In addition to the important evidence gleaned from these systems, the use of linked administrative data along with the infrastructure to maintain and use an SLDS develops the capacity to replace what may have previously been manual reporting. By implementing advanced computing power and incorporating valuable feedback from key stakeholders, the process of generating regular metrics has been transformed to render them almost instantly available. Gone are the days that required weeks or even months of work to develop reports; now, the power of an SLDS enables real-time data analysis and streamlined reporting.

Enhances productivity and evidence-based practices. Metrics are also expanded beyond what was previously required for federal reporting to strengthen insights into service delivery and outcomes. With less time spent on cumbersome reporting tasks, public employees can focus on using the evidence derived from the SLDS to improve existing services and develop new, innovative initiatives. This time-saving aspect not only enhances productivity but creates a dynamic environment where evidence-based practices sit at the forefront of decision-making processes.

Expanding the use of emerging technologies and analytics. The use of artificial intelligence and/or machine learning presents an exciting opportunity to effectively enhance the public sector's ability to use administrative data, although it is in its infancy for this purpose. Some success has occurred through the development of predictive analytics, allowing state agencies to compare current data to historic trends, determine potential risks for program participants, or assess broader policy implications. Using AI to promote warning systems that keep policymakers informed can also help to quickly and efficiently target resources to ensure successful outcomes.

By leveraging advanced analytics, time-saving artificial intelligence tools, and predictive modeling and/or warning systems, policymakers can proactively identify potential issues and trends, enabling them to take preemptive actions and design targeted interventions to address emerging challenges effectively. The development and implementation of progress benchmarks allows for continuous evaluation of the effectiveness of policies and programs. This feedback loop ensures that public services are continuously improved based on real-time data for more efficient and impactful outcomes.

Using Data as a Hub for Policy Innovation

The impact of these systems grows significantly as more agencies participate and data usage expands, making them hubs of innovation that enhance policymaking through predictive analytics, warning systems, and progress benchmarks. States that have recognized this potential by prioritizing sustainable funding and providing support for SLDS implementation continue to reap these benefits and will keep doing so in the future. Forward-thinking states can embrace these emerging systems and establish sustainable platforms for the next generation of public services.

Participation in a state's SLDS should extend to all relevant stakeholders, including state agencies that may not have been included in the initial development of education and earnings systems. More holistic participation in an SLDS allows for better evidence to understand individual experiences, barriers, and the policies that better support agencies. Building a multistakeholder approach will require agencies to collaborate, share data, and develop meaningful and sustainable partnerships. Through this collaboration, stakeholders can ensure that the data is used effectively to inform policy decisions and improve program outcomes.

Benefits of Using Shared Data Systems

Benefits of shared data systems are not limited to only those agencies that created them and it opens the opportunity for expanded public service across agencies. Mathematica's recent Education-to-Workforce Indicator Framework[3] highlights types of questions that can be answered by linked administrative data. Among many others, these indicators include access to in-demand career training, access to health and social supports, school and workplace diversity, and economic mobility. New Jersey's Benefits of Education report used SLDS data to highlight the experiences of students in the state, as well as the return on investment of postsecondary education to individuals and society.[4] The development of robust state systems that can address these questions for their stakeholders will be critical to the future of education and career service delivery directly, with added understanding of effects from programs such as public health, nutrition programs, and more.

Use of an SLDS informs policymaking to improve outcomes. With an operational SLDS, system operators can automate reporting of important metrics to create feedback loops to improve policy. For instance, predictive analytics can help to identify students who are at risk of dropping out of school or not completing a degree on time, warning systems can notify policymakers of potential concerns with a particular program or policy, and benchmarks can help to track program outcomes over time and adjust implementation as needed. By developing a robust SLDS, the public sector gains the ability to make evidence-based decisions, resulting in more efficient policy implementation and effective outcomes for the people they serve.

LOOKING FORWARD

As more states embark on their development of SLDS, they encounter certain challenges that need to be addressed for optimal implementation.

- **Sharing experiences and insights.** Inclusive governance and sustainability have emerged as critical factors for the successful establishment of these systems. Collaborative meetings and events like the annual SLDS Best Practices Conference,[5] organized by the ED for participating states, play a crucial role in sharing experiences and insights. During such gatherings, representatives discuss strategies to engage stakeholders effectively, create research agendas, build, and update necessary infrastructure, and disseminate results to inform policymaking.

- **Consistent and dedicated investment.** A continued challenge that many state systems face remains the need for consistent and dedicated funding. Despite receiving grants from ED for this purpose, many states find the process complex, demanding, and a strain on already limited resources. Sustaining the momentum and ensuring ongoing support becomes a vital concern for long-term success. Budget constraints and competing priorities pose challenges to making the significant investments necessary in building innovative and sustainable systems. Without dedicated funding, early investments to build a states' SLDS could stagnate, limiting their ability to reach their potential in informing policy and advancing current practices.

- **Building and maintaining trust.** In addition to funding challenges, other barriers influence the successful implementation of an SLDS. Building and maintaining trust among various agencies and stakeholders is essential for data sharing and collaboration. Establishing a robust governance framework that addresses these concerns while promoting transparency and accountability can foster trust and encourage data-sharing collaboration. New Jersey has moved toward this goal through a multistakeholder approach[6] to data governance.

- **Raising awareness.** Furthermore, raising awareness about the benefits of an SLDS is vital among policymakers and the public. Educating stakeholders about the power of data-driven policymaking and how SLDS can facilitate evidence-based decisions will garner support for these initiatives and promote informed decision making across all levels of governance.

- **Ensuring sustained leadership support.** Additionally, ensuring sustained political support and leadership is crucial for the continuity and prioritization of SLDS efforts. By fostering a nonpartisan approach to data utilization in policymaking, states can ensure that SLDS initiatives remain stable and serve as a solid foundation for long-term governance, transcending political cycles and driving transformative changes in evidence-based policymaking.

The SLDS is a relatively new tool, but its potential to revolutionize government service delivery is tremendous. As these systems evolve, they become even more potent in improving the lives of citizens. To ensure the continued growth of SLDS, government must invest in their maintenance and long-term sustainability. This includes offering startup funds for states that haven't yet developed their SLDS and dedicating regular funding to maintain and enhance existing systems. To drive awareness and use of these systems, additional funding and initiatives should focus on informing the public and shaping policies based on SLDS data. Lessons learned from this experience can provide models for governments to build on in adapting current or developing new ways to capitalize on rich stores of available administrative data across multiple program areas.

To build on the potential of SLDS in developing policy for leveraging administrative data more generally, both the federal government and individual states must make strategic investments in maintaining and sustaining the extensive infrastructure that has already been developed. By proactively addressing these challenges and investing in the necessary resources, we can empower evidence-based policymaking and create a data-driven landscape that truly serves the needs of citizens and propels the public sector into a more effective and efficient future.

Stephanie Walsh, *PhD, is the Assistant Director of Research at the Heldrich Center for Workforce Development. She earned her doctorate in planning and public policy at Rutgers University. Her research interests focus on how data can inform public programs and policies to better support service delivery and improve individual outcomes.*

Kevin Dehmer *is Executive Director of the Heldrich Center for Workforce Development. He is responsible for executive management and day-to-day oversight of research, administration, communications, program development, technical assistance, policy implementation, client services, and project operations.*

Endnotes

1   Figlio, David, Krzysztof Karbownik, and Kjell G. Salvanes. "Education research and administrative data." In *Handbook of the economics of education*, vol. 5, pp. 75-138. Elsevier, 2016.

2   Black, Sandra E., Paul J. Devereux, and Kjell G. Salvanes. "Why the apple doesn't fall far: Understanding intergenerational transmission of human capital." *American Economic Review*, 95, no. 1 (2005): 437-449.

3   Education-to-Workforce Indicator Framework, Mathematica, 2022. (https://www.mathematica.org/projects/education-to-workforce-indicator-framework).

4   Simone, Sean, PhD, Ahmad Salman Zafar, Kristine Joy Bacani, and Jessica Cruz-Nagoski. Benefits of Education in New Jersey, Heldrich Center for Workforce Development, January 2023. (https://njeeds.org/products-research/benefits-of-education-in-new-jersey/).

5   Statewide Longitudinal Data Systems: Best Practices Conference: https://slds.ed.gov/services/PDCService.svc/GetPDCDocumentFile?fileId=43934.

6   Walsh, Stephanie, and Shashi Yellambhatla. New Jersey's Longitudinal Governance: A multi-stakeholder process. Heldrich Center for Workforce Development, February 23, 2023. https://www.heldrich.rutgers.edu/sites/default/files/2023-03/NJ _ New _ Jersey.pdf.

PART III | **ON FUTURE READINESS: INSIGHTS FROM EXPERTS**

PERFORMANCE

Chapter Eleven

Toward More Useful Federal Oversight

By Shelley Metzenbaum
The BETTER Project

INTRODUCTION

Well-executed oversight is an invaluable aspect of government operations. It complements program and cross-program implementation by increasing the likelihood that government spending and actions realize their intended benefit.

In the future, federal oversight can be made more useful to more users for more purposes. Continually evolving technologies make it easier and more affordable than ever to collect, analyze, and use oversight data and analyses to anticipate, detect, prepare for, prevent, and respond more quickly, fully, and successfully to problems. Evolving technologies and analytic approaches can deliver more insights not just to federal programs but also to federal delivery partners to help them anticipate, prevent, and address problems and pursue improvement opportunities more pro-actively[1] and more strategically, addressing the most serious problems and opportunities before proceeding to other key actions. In addition, lessons from experience and well-designed trials can reveal better ways to communicate oversight findings and other evidence in order to realize better outcomes and operational quality while building understanding of and trust in government.

Those doing oversight are beginning to tap evolving technologies. What lessons are they learning, technology-linked and otherwise? What barriers are they encountering? What new oversight approaches are worth testing and assessing? Finally, who does, can, and should search for and share lessons learned and build new knowledge and capacity for more useful oversight?

This chapter explores these questions. It seeks to engage others in asking, answering, and acting to adopt more useful approaches to oversight that improve government performance on multiple dimensions.

What is oversight?

Oversight, as defined in this chapter, is work done by those *not* charged with daily and longer-term program operations, but rather work done to look for and report on problems and opportunities and make recommendations regarding them. Oversight supplements but does not supplant internal agency evaluation and goal and program management.[2] Oversight takes many forms, such as investigation, field observation, hotline calls, and data collection and analyses. It includes the search for promising as well as problematic practices.

Why is oversight needed?

An important objective of government oversight is to prevent and penalize fraud and corruption. Fraud and corruption can originate outside government,[3] within government,[4] and by government contractors.[5] Oversight aids the search to find, prevent, and penalize these problems.

Oversight also brings attention to poor work quality and operational problems.[6] It can reveal organizational culture problems,[7] and spotlight government duplication, fragmentation, and overlap.[8] Oversight illuminates issues needing but not getting attention. It reduces the risk that programs run on autopilot instead of continually searching for ways to do better. By finding relevant peer performance, oversight can play an innovation-encouraging role, similar to how private sector competitors play.

Who conducts oversight?

Many conduct oversight in the U.S. federal government: Congressional committees, Government Accountability Office (GAO), agency inspectors general (IGs), IG networks, and program and regional offices. Plus, federal grant recipients receiving $750,000 or more a year must hire private sector auditors to conduct annual "single audits."[9]

Congress has authorized GAO and IGs to conduct oversight. GAO originally focused on savings and efficiency,[10] and now looks for other government improvement opportunities. Inspectors General function "as independent government watchdogs who seek out fraud, waste, and abuse and who promote effective management in federal programs."[11] Agency program offices often conduct oversight of those they fund, complementing other program activities such as getting dollars out and helping grant recipients learn from each other and collaborate. The ways program offices conduct oversight often varies. Cross-agency oversight is also done, much of it through the congressionally created Council of the Inspectors General on Integrity and Efficiency (CIGIE).

How are oversight findings used?

Oversight findings encourage specific actions to correct specific problems. GAO and IGs both track their recommendations to encourage corrective action. GAO also periodically updates a high-risk list to encourage action in high-need areas. Oversight findings also suggest ways to improve, as when GAO identifies agencies reducing improper payments to help other agencies.[12]

Different situations call for different types of oversight. Intentionally fraudulent use of government funds obviously warrants severe punishment. Oversight findings of poor implementation practices, however, often warrant assistance, not punishment, except when recalcitrance to making needed change is evident.

Who can and should use oversight findings?

Congress, agency, and program leaders are target audiences for oversight information. Oversight can also help those working on and supporting the frontline and others.

More attention needs to be given to "uses" and "users" of oversight findings. Questions then need to be asked about whether those users are aware of and can find oversight findings, and whether they view such findings as useful for anticipating and preventing problems, addressing those that do occur, and improving outcomes. The Office of Head Start (OHS) at the Department of Health and Human Services talks about using monitoring findings to inform OHS but not to help help children and families in Head Start programs.[13] Presumably, Head Start programs are also an important audience for monitoring findings, including findings from the "Promising Practices Pilot" announced in OHS's FY2023 monitoring protocols.[14]

Adopting an agile and user-centered design approach like that used to upgrade USASpending.gov[15] can contribute to more useful oversight. Indeed, the Pandemic Response Accountability Committee of CIGIE (PRAC) released a tool kit to support agile oversight.[16] New technologies make agile, user-centered design more feasible than ever. Websites can invite interested parties to opt for updates and note their areas of interest. Also, online platforms facilitate fast, iterative feedback that can support continuous improvement.

The following cases describe efforts to make oversight more useful, suggesting how new technologies and sharing lessons learned might contribute to more useful future oversight.

Case 1: Recovery Act

Implementation of the Recovery Act suggests better ways to use and communicate oversight information. A small White House-based Recovery Act implementation office supporting then Vice President Biden managed Recovery Act implementation. GAO commended this effort for: (1) strong support of top leaders, (2) centrally situated collaborative governance, (3) use of networks and agreements to share information and work toward common goals, and (4) adjustments to, and innovations in, usual approaches to conducting oversight (e.g., increased use of upfront risk assessments, real time information, earlier communication of audit findings, and use of advanced data analytics).[17]

Congress also legislated a Recovery Act Accountability and Transparency Board (RAT Board) for oversight. The RAT Board launched Recovery.gov, building and improving on the existing mapping platform of another agency. Mapping this facilitated seeing where Recovery Act funds were initially allocated,[18] and mapping increased public interest in communities. The public also became more aware of how federal spending might affect them. GAO praised this website for: clear purpose, using social networking tools to garner interest, tailoring website to audience needs, and obtaining stakeholder input during design.[19]

Future agency and oversight spending maps might go beyond mapping spending to show spending options under consideration, progress made, and post-spending impact in each location. Spending on physical space projects, for example, might link to photos showing interim and final progress and to data and descriptions about spending purposes and impact.

GAO and others[20] have captured some valuable lessons learned from Recovery Act implementation to inform future congressional action and agency implementation, but these studies have missed some important lessons. For example, Congress appropriated $84 million for the RAT Board but did not fund a program implementation office. Most employees of the small RAT Board implementation office that GAO praised were "detailed" or borrowed from other agencies. It remains unclear whether this is a good precedent. Also, Recovery.gov disappeared when the RAT Board ceased operations. Government neither sustained nor archived the site, eliminating not only an online platform for other agencies to use and improve but also lessons about the website's functionality. The White House created the Government Accountability and Transparency Board, which reflected on and issued a set of recommendations.[21] However, there appears to be no entity that tracks action on the recommendations made by this board. Nor does any entity routinely learn from cross-agency experiences to recommend authorities and resources needed to manage cross-agency implementation well.

Case 2: Federal Emergency Management Administration

The Federal Emergency Management Administration (FEMA) has done pioneering work to make oversight information more useful. A newly created, FEMA audit office converted IG, GAO, program, and grant single audit findings stored as PDFs (much in the Federal Audit Clearinghouse) into consolidated data, housed in a single, searchable database. FEMA staff used natural language processing complemented by human intelligence to note which regulatory authority auditors cited for problems, allowing FEMA to sort audit findings by keywords in chapters, sections, and paragraphs of regulatory text.

FEMA staff also noted date, location, dollar amounts, closure status, and audit teams for each data item. It used these data to create a Compliance Dashboard succinctly visualizing current and historic compliance patterns.[22] The dashboard includes a bubble chart showing the most common (but not necessarily the most serious) compliance problems, trend graphs for different subsets, and color-varying maps suggesting persistent and unresolved problems. This enables comparisons across time, location, and audit teams. The figures trigger focused follow-up discussions to decide appropriate follow-up actions. FEMA leaders and those running FEMA training efforts receive the dashboards; a publicly shared version of the dashboard shows results including problems trending downward, suggesting that this information is being used to prevent and reduce noncompliance.[23]

FEMA has not yet tried to access other data sources to consider if and how its compliance requirements align with real-world risks. Nor has the agency made the dashboard public. Nonetheless, this approach to oversight information suggests a future approach all federal agencies can take to manage oversight, consolidating historic findings into a searchable data base and developing better ways to collect future information to facilitate mapping, trend analyses, noncompliance analyses, and other action-informing visualizations.

Case 3: Pandemic Response Accountability Committee

Congress created the PRAC when it passed the Coronavirus Aid, Relief, and Economic Security (CARES) Act. PRAC's Pandemic Analytics Center of Excellence (PACE) recently embraced a big data approach. Its projects suggest the enormous potential of tapping data from outside the implementing agency. PACE analyzed over 33 million applications for Small Business Administration (SBA) CARES Act funding together with publicly available Social Security Administration (SSA) information to identify suspected invalid or unassigned SSNs. PACE then asked SSA to verify those SSNs. SSA informed the PRAC that over 221,000 of those SSNs were not issued by SSA nor did they match applicant-provided birth information—suggesting potential identity fraud.[24] This PACE analysis suggests one kind of analysis that oversight bodies can do to help federal agencies and their state, local, territorial, and tribal delivery partners anticipate and prevent problems.

PRAC had difficulty accessing SSA data in a timely way to do this early-warning analyses.[25] This suggests a need for an "after action" review to understand the kinds of data-sharing arrangements needed to enable more timely, useful future oversight. Related questions warranting attention include:

- Who does these sorts of "after action" reviews and recommends action to Congress and Executive Branch leaders?

- Who tracks and encourages follow-up on recommendations?

- What funding is needed to do this well?

LOOKING FORWARD

Given oversight purposes and what they imply about uses and users of oversight findings, these three mini cases suggest the following future action:

1. **Treat oversight findings as data for generating greater insights to anticipate and more strategically prevent problems, address problems, and pursue opportunities.** Careful thought is needed on how to store and share oversight findings to make analyses easier. Lessons can come not just from those doing oversight but also from the many government programs that collect and analyze data to aid planning, preparedness, prevention, response, and recovery. Thought also needs to be given to whether and how to convert past oversight findings to a more analyzable form, data standards, data dictionaries, and data-sharing agreements. More thought is also needed about how to tag collected information to facilitate searching and sorting across oversight findings by categories such as outcome objectives, process types, populations served, time, location, and incentive structure.

2. **Collect and share oversight data in as close to real time as possible.** In addition to PRAC's agile oversight tool, a White House memo on the Infrastructure Investment and Jobs Act strongly urges more proactive approaches.[26] Timelier and more spatially and geographically frequent data tend to support more proactive approaches.

3. **Analyze oversight findings and other data within and across agencies.** Data analyses to assess oversight findings across programs and agencies for patterns, similarities, variations, relationships, clusters, trends, positive and negative outliers, and anomalies across time and subsets can help to prevent and more strategically respond to problems that occur; such data can also reveal opportunities for improvement, including opportunities for cross-program scale economies. These kinds of data can also aid identification of causal factors to influence precursor events useful as warning signs.

4. **Look for better and promising practices along with problems and risks.** Oversight should include the search for practices associated with progress within and across agencies. These should include finding better products and services likely to help those served, regulated, and protected as well as better internal practices, such as useful metrics,

report generators (old-fashioned and AI-supported), and incentive structures. The search for better practices also requires looking beyond aver-
ages to variation to understand how different situations affect efficacy.
And, cross-program analyses of risks and contextual changes affecting
multiple programs promise efficiencies. Oversight bodies can do this
cross-program analyses, or if not they can suggest how to get it done.

5. **Continually learn from experience and well-designed trials and build
    capacity to learn within and across programs.** Oversight can support
    continuous learning about effective practices within and across programs.
    Some of these practices could include programs sharing outcome objec-
    tives and programs using similar implementation processes such as
    benefits processing. Oversight can also support the creation of shared
    evidence libraries to house information on shared outcomes and similar
    processes. It could encourage iterative trials to improve the functional-
    ity and cut the costs of evidence libraries (as NASA uses NIH's PubMed
    platform) and other knowledge-sharing tools.[27] Where appropriate, over-
    sight can encourage shared learning agendas.

6. **Successfully communicate oversight findings, lessons learned, and
    needs with important users.** CIGIE's Oversight.gov is a promising step
    forward in communicating oversight findings. More useful oversight also
    requires attention to target users, and whether they know about and
    are easily and affordably able to access, understand, and apply relevant
    oversight and other needed information. This, of course, requires care-
    ful thought as to key users, their relative priority, and their information
    needs. Oversight can share relevant information about users of informa-
    tion and other evidence and effective ways to communicate with those
    users. It can encourage shared trials to find better ways to communicate
    to different users, and to strengthen understanding of skills needed to
    communicate findings and lessons learned successfully.

7. **Sufficiently resource data design, collection, analyses, communication,
    and active management within and across agencies.** The six activities rec-
    ommended above need to be encouraged and actively resourced by Con-
    gress and leaders, within and across agencies, which oversight can inform.

Moving forward on actions suggested above will require tackling specific
challenges, including:

1. **Data standards confusion.** Data standards strengthen improvement-
    informing insights so Congress has frequently mandated data
    standards—in the DATA Act of 2014, GREAT Act of 2019, Financial
    Data Transparency Act of 2022, and other laws. How these efforts
    fit together, planned next steps, and how to engage is confusing. The
    Federal Data Strategy's Action 2 indicated its intent to align multiple
    data standard efforts.[28] The status of this strategy is, however, unclear.
    Alignment, public information about planned next steps and why they
    were chosen, and external engagement would be helpful.

2. **Entities responsible for learning across agencies and finding and shar-
    ing lessons learned about shared risks, priority users, are unclear.** The
    three cases discussed above suggest the value of more systematically
    searching for and successfully sharing oversight findings and other evi-
    dence, across agencies and time. Congress ought to consider and decide
    who should lead cross-agency learning and the resources needed to do
    continuous learning and improvement well. CIGIE and GAO members,
    sufficiently resourced, would obviously need to be involved—as should
    other potential oversight and evidence users, including frontline workers.

3. **Barriers to user-centered design and data sharing.** More useful over-
    sight and evidence requires better understanding of user needs and
    experience. Unfortunately, barriers exist to gathering useful feedback
    about government's knowledge-sharing efforts such as webinars and
    evidence libraries. Real and perceived barriers, such as Paperwork
    Reduction Act, may also impede data sharing.[29] Government needs fre-
    quent feedback for agile and effective action about ongoing oversight,
    to identify barriers to user-centered design and recommend ways to
    remove them is needed.

There is reason for optimism despite these challenges. This chapter seeks to
foster ideas about how to make government oversight more useful for more
users. This requires finding new ways to do and use oversight and other
information—in more effective, efficient, and fair ways, to improve outcomes,
operational quality, and public understanding of and trust in government.

Shelley H. Metzenbaum, *The BETTER Project (Bringing Everyone Together to Enhance Results), was OMB Associate Director for performance and personnel management, founding President of The Volcker Alliance, and head of EPA Regional Operations & State/Local Relations. She teaches and writes about using goals and data to improve outcomes without making people afraid, compromising performance.*

Endnotes

1   White House," Memorandum for the Heads of Executive Departments and Agencies re Advancing Effective Stewardship of Taxpayer Resources and Outcomes in the Implementation of the Infrastructure Investment and Jobs Act, M-22-12, https://www.whitehouse.gov/wp-content/uploads/2022/04/M-22-12.pdf.

2   Honorable Greg Friedman, U.S. Department of Energy Inspector General, 1998-2015.

3   U.S. Pandemic Responsibility Accountability Committee, Fraud Alert: PRAC Identifies $5.4 Billion in Potentially Fraudulent Pandemic Loans Obtained Using Over 69,000 Questionable Social Security Numbers, https://www.pandemicoversight.gov/sites/default/files/2023-01/PRAC%20fraud%20alert%20on%20potential%20SSN%20fraud _ 1.pdf.

4   McWhirter, Cameron, "Former Mississippi Human Services Director Pleads Guilty to Charges Related to Welfare Scandal," *Wall Street Journal*, September 2022, https://www.wsj.com/articles/former-mississippi-human-services-director-pleads-guilty-to-charges-related-to-welfare-scandal-11663887132.

5   Associated Press, "General manager of electrical company pleads guilty to defrauding MBTA operator, Keolis," WBUR. June 14, 2023, https://www.wbur.org/news/2023/06/14/john-rafferty-fraud-boston-mbta-rail.

6   Johnson, Charles A. and Kathryn E. Newcomer, U.S. Inspectors General. Brookings, 2020. pp. 184-193.

7   Sparrow, Malcolm, *Handcuffed*. pp.12-17 (Kindle). Brookings 2016.

8   U.S. Government Accountability Office, 2023 Annual Report: Additional Opportunities to Reduce Fragmentation, Overlap, and Duplication and Achieve Billions of Dollars in Financial Benefits, June 14, 2023. GAO-23-10608, https://www.gao.gov/duplication-cost-savings.

9   Code of Federal Regulations, Subpart F, Audit Requirements, https://www.ecfr.gov/current/title-2/subtitle-A/chapter-II/part-200/subpart-F.

10   https://www.gao.gov/about.

11   Johnson and Newcomer, p. xv.

12   U.S. Government Accountability Office. Improper Payments: Programs Reporting Reductions Had Taken Corrective Actions That Shared Common Features, June 30, 2023. GAO-23-106585, https://www.gao.gov/products/gao-23-106585.

13   U.S. Office of Head Start, Fiscal Year (FY) 2023 Head Start Monitoring Protocols, https://eclkc.ohs.acf.hhs.gov/federal-monitoring/article/fiscal-year-fy-2023-head-start-monitoring-protocols.

14   U.S. Office of Head Start. FY23 Monitoring Kickoff, September 29, 2022, https://eclkc.ohs.acf.hhs.gov/sites/default/files/video/attachments/fy2023-monitoring-kickoff-slides.pdf.

15   National Academy of Public Administration, DATA Act Implementation: The First Government-Wide Agile Project, April 30, 2020, https://napawash.org/grand-challenges-blog/data-act-implementation-the-first-government-wide-agile-project.

16   Pandemic Response Accountability Committee Agile Products Toolkit, https://www.pandemicoversight.gov/media/file/agile-products-toolkit2022pdf.

17   U.S. Government Accountability Office. Recovery Act: Grant Implementation Experiences Offer Lessons for Accountability and Transparency, GAO-14-219, https://www.gao.gov/assets/gao-14-219.pdf.

18   Although not where sub-grantees and sub-contractors eventually spent those funds, a functionality that needs to be developed.

19   U.S. Government Accountability Office. Recovery Act: Grant Implementation Experiences Offer Lessons for Accountability and Transparency, GAO-14-219, https://www.gao.gov/assets/gao-14-219.pdf.

20   Fine, Glenn. Fighting fraud, waste, and abuse—the 2009 Recovery Act, Brookings, February 11, 2022, https://www.brookings.edu/articles/fighting-fraud-waste-and-abuse-the-2009-recovery-act/#:~:text=The%20Recovery%20Board%20was%20led%20by%20a%20full-time,in%20funding%20and%20employed%20approximately%2035%20staff%20members.

21   U.S. Government Accountability and Transparency Board, Report and Recommendations to the President, December 2011, https://obamawhitehouse.archives.gov/sites/default/files/gat _ board _ december _ 2011 _ report _ and _ recommendations.pdf.

22   Federal Emergency Management Administration, Compliance Dashboard presented to National Academy of Public Administration Grants Management Symposium, https://s3.us-west-2.amazonaws.com/napa-2021/Grants-Management-Symposium/FEMA _ COD _ Handout.pdf.

23   For more background on this example, see Metzenbaum, Shelley, *Federal Grants Management: Improving Operational Quality*, IBM Center for The Business of Government, 2021, pp. 11-15, https://www.businessofgovernment.org/sites/default/files/Improving%20Operational%20Quality.pdf#page=11.

24   U.S. Pandemic Responsibility Accountability Committee, Fraud Alert: PRAC Identifies $5.4 Billion in Potentially Fraudulent Pandemic Loans Obtained Using Over 69,000 Questionable Social Security Numbers, https://www.pandemicoversight.gov/sites/default/files/2023-01/PRAC%20fraud%20alert%20on%20potential%20SSN%20fraud _ 1.pdf.

25   Buble, Courtney, 'These were not normal times': A former watchdog reflects on COVID-19 oversight, Government Executive, June 30, 2023, https://www.govexec.com/oversight/2023/06/these-were-not-normal-times-former-watchdog-reflects-covid-19-oversight/388102/.

26   White House, Memorandum for the Heads of Executive Departments and Agencies re Advancing Effective Stewardship of Taxpayer Resources and Outcomes in the Implementation of the Infrastructure Investment and Jobs Act, M-22-12, https://www.whitehouse.gov/wp-content/uploads/2022/04/M-22-12.pdf.

27   Chief Financial Officers Council, Managing for Results: The Performance Management Playbook for Federal Awarding Agencies, April 2020, p. 35, https://www.cfo.gov/wp-content/uploads/2021/Managing-for-Results-Performance-Management-Playbook-for-Federal-Awarding-Agencies.pdf.

28   Federal Data Strategy, Leveraging Data as a Strategic Asset, 2020 Action Plan, https://strategy.data.gov/action-plan/#action-20-develop-a-data-standards-repository.

29   Womer, Jonathan and Kathy Stack. Blending and Braiding Funds: Opportunities to Strengthen State and Local Data and Evaluation Capacity in Human Service, SSRN, April 13, 2023, https://papers.ssrn.com/sol3/papers.cfm?abstract _ id=4403532.

Chapter Twelve

Future of Payment Integrity within the U.S. Federal Government

By Renata Miskell
U.S. Department of the Treasury

INTRODUCTION

Paying the right person, in the right amount, at the right time—from Social Security benefits to tax refund payments—constitutes a bedrock of trust in government. Disbursing payments, whether via check or (ideally) direct deposit, is one of the most direct ways that the federal government interacts with the public. It also represents one of the primary levers that the federal government uses to provide a safety net to vulnerable populations, promote economic prosperity, and ensure national security. Put simply, payment integrity stands as one of the most important functions that government performs to promote the public good.

Payment integrity can strengthen trust in government by reducing improper payments and preventing fraud in federal programs. An improper payment is defined by the most recent payment integrity legislation, the Payment Integrity Information Act (PIIA) of 2019,[1] as a payment that should not have been made.[2] Improper payments occur when funds go to the wrong recipient, the right recipient receives the wrong amount; absent documentation to support a payment. As such, improper payments may not ultimately result in a monetary loss to the government. While not all improper payments are due to fraud and not all improper payments will ultimately represent a monetary loss to the government, all improper payments degrade the integrity of government programs and compromise citizens' trust in government.

This chapter explores a vision that would empower agencies and federally funded programs, including state administered programs, to use data proactively in promoting payment integrity. This vision involves collaborating with federal and state agencies to share data and provide actionable business solutions to transform the identification, prevention, and recovery of improper payments; and to mitigate the effects of fraud. It also emphasizes a pivot from compliance to prevention-focused strategies, promoting the use of data and analytics and collaboration across government and the private commercial sectors. Emerging technologies like artificial intelligence and machine learning are crucial catalysts for this transformation, enhancing data analysis, streamlining processes, facilitating data sharing and the reuse of data, and improving fraud detection and prevention; all while prioritizing data privacy and security.

From Recovery to Prevention

For American citizens, government must get payments right. A late unemployment insurance payment—or worse, one intercepted in an act of fraud—can have severe consequences for a family relying on that assistance during a time of financial hardship. Similarly, if tax dollars are wasted on duplicate payments or payments to ineligible recipients, public trust in government will erode, and taxpayers and lawmakers will be less willing to fund future financial assistance programs. Moreover, when the federal government reissues a payment to correct an improper payment, it bears significant additional operational costs, on top of the inconvenience and added burden to the recipient.

The government recently saw the positive effects of federal disaster support in the form of loans and direct payments delivered in record time. The U.S. Department of the Treasury (Treasury) rapidly issued three waves of direct relief payments, or Economic Impact Payments (EIP), during the COVID-19 pandemic. The amounts of these payments dwarfed the size of similar historic efforts and were delivered in record speed, including a third round of payments where Treasury issued 174 million payments totaling $407 billion within a few days of the enactment of authorizing legislation.

At the same time, unprecedented spending in response to the COVID-19 pandemic exposed vulnerabilities in federal and state government payment systems, leading to increased fraud, and exacerbating long-standing payment integrity challenges. For example, in a rush to quickly get relief to businesses and nonprofits, the Small Business Administration (SBA) disbursed over 4.5 million potentially fraudulent loans and grants via the Paycheck Protection Program (PPP) and Economic Injury Disaster Loan (EIDL) program totaling over $200 billion. Despite substantial oversight and law enforcement efforts, only $30 billion in EIDL and PPP funds have been seized or returned to SBA as of June 2023.[3]

The federal government needs to do more to manage risk and shift the focus from recovery to prevention. No one can predict when the next large-scale emergency or disaster will occur, but when they do, fraudsters will look to exploit weaknesses in government assistance programs. Just as Treasury issues payments rapidly to those in need, it also needs to stop fraudsters and improper payments more broadly in near real-time.

Current Issues and Challenges

Over the past two decades, the focus of laws and regulations governing the identification and recovery of improper payments has evolved from reporting to emphasize prevention and promoting the use of centralized services. Despite positive advancements in legislation and policy as well as improvements in compliance reporting and overall transparency as federal government spending has increased over the past decade, so have improper payments.

According to the Government Accountability Office (GAO), since 2003, when federal agencies began keeping track of improper payments, cumulative improper payment estimates total almost $2.4 trillion.[4] The payment accuracy rate has hovered around 95 percent, with a high of 96.5 percent in 2013 and a low of 92.8 percent in 2021. Five programs account for 78 percent of all improper payments;[5] however, approximately 92 percent of overpayments in high-priority programs were beyond the control of a single agency.[6] While this was a decrease from the FY2021 estimated total of $281 billion, the payment accuracy rate remains unchanged at 95 percent (see Table 1).

Table 1: Improper Payment Volume & Accuracy Rate over the Past Decade

Source: U.S. Government Accountability Office

Persistent challenges make it difficult for any single federal program or agency to move the needle in advancing payment integrity. The urgency to "get money out the door" in an emergency is a challenge for federal programs, and so are their efforts to access and use data in a timely manner to prevent improper payments and fraud. Eligibility criteria such as death and income are recurring payment integrity challenges because of the difficulty in accessing verification data. Insufficient data analytics for fraud prevention only exacerbate the problem. Moreover, misaligned incentives and complex systems limit accountability. While government has advanced in its ability to estimate improper payments, reporting is after the fact and not integrated into the pre-payment and pre-award processes.

Vision for Advancing Payment Integrity

The best way to reduce fraud and improper payments is to prevent them from happening at all, by performing risk assessments and building in proper internal controls at the front end when designing and executing federal programs. Guidance from OMB[7] and GAO,[8] as well as resources that promote best practices,[9] emphasize the importance of assessing risk and accessing and using quality information and data to detect, prevent, and monitor improper payments and fraud. Given the importance of timely access to data, the use of technology and advanced analytics are crucial catalysts for also advancing payment integrity.

Imagine if the federal government could enable agencies and federally funded state administered (FFSA) programs to prevent and detect fraud and improper payments in real-time throughout the payment lifecycle—from pre-award to pre-payment, through sub-award, to post payment processes. As the primary disbursing agency responsible for over 90 percent of federal payments, Treasury has developed a bold vison to empower government to use data proactively in promoting payment integrity. The vision involves collaborating with federally funded and state-administered programs to provide actionable solutions to transform the identification, prevention, and recovery of improper payments and to mitigate the effects of fraud.

This vision mirrors the experience the public has engaging in financial transactions through banks or when using credit cards. Private sector financial institutions and payment networks arguably have greater access to capital, more flexibility to innovate, and fewer constraints and dependencies than government agencies. However, Treasury has three distinct advantages—scale, scope, and authority—that can springboard the federal government's ability to advance payment integrity. In FY2022, Treasury's Bureau of the Fiscal Service (Fiscal Service) securely disbursed approximately 1.4 billion payments totaling more than $5.3 trillion. These payments went to 100+ million individuals and entities, with 96 percent disbursed electronically, creating a modern, seamless, and cost-effective payment experience.[10] Treasury's central disbursing authority enables it to touch virtually every aspect of the payment lifecycle. Just as Treasury has accelerated the speed with which government can make payments, so too can it accelerate the government's ability to prevent fraud and reduce improper payments by leveraging technology and advanced analytics.

Three Strategies for Advancing Payment Integrity

Payment integrity relies on a complex web of stakeholders, systems, processes, and controls throughout the payment lifecycle. Advancing Treasury's vision of real-time detection and prevention will require a digital transformation throughout the payment lifecycle. Three key strategies can advance this vision: focusing on prevention, embracing best practices, and strengthening partnerships.

Focus on prevention

The best way to reduce the fraud and improper payments rate is to make sure they do not happen in the first place. Shifting to real-time detection and prevention is the building block on which the other strategies rest. This foundational focus makes moving forward on payment integrity possible.

Payment integrity as a service. To achieve real time detection and prevention, government needs to move away from siloed, manual processes and shift to digitized, modular payment integrity capabilities using cloud technology. Digitization of payment integrity activities is a force multiplier, enabling government to meet the enormous scale, scope, and complexity of federal award and payment processes. A digital operating model enables rapid learning that can drive continuous improvement, expedite connections across the payment lifecycle, create the ability to scale quickly as funding increases, and efficiently implement payment integrity capabilities as new programs are established. This also helps prevent improper payments before they go out the door.

Just like the "All Electronic Treasury" initiative that converted millions of paper check payments to electronic payments over the past decade, this transformative shift to a digital operating model as a service is achievable with sustained leadership commitment. Treasury's Bureau of the Fiscal Service has jump started such an effort. Since 2011, it has been developing and enhancing the Do Not Pay (DNP) Working System (previously named DNP Business Center) to assist agencies in identifying and preventing improper payments.

Moreover, with the recently established Office of Payment Integrity, the Fiscal Service has brought together detection and prevention services with payment and post-payment functions. This has already enabled a more holistic and integrated set of payment integrity solutions. For example, in FY2021, the Fiscal Service launched its commercial Account Verification Service (AVS) pilot. The AVS's main purpose was to verify bank account status (e.g., open or closed) prior to payment in advance of the third round of EIP and the Advance Child Tax Credit (ACTC). By the end of FY2022, the Fiscal Service screened 2.7 million accounts through AVS, preventing $130 million of improper payments. In addition to expanding access to AVS to FFSA programs via DNP, Treasury can build on the success of using commercial and government data sources to provide actionable payment integrity services.

Leverage emerging technology and advanced analytics. Treasury continues to modernize DNP's platform to scale and optimize data pipelines, support artificial intelligence (AI) and machine learning (ML) processes, and advance analytics toward a fully digitized "payment integrity as a service." Emerging technologies like AI and ML are crucial catalysts for this transformation, enhancing data analysis, streamlining processes, facilitating the reuse of data, and improving fraud detection and prevention. As the central federal disbursing agency, Treasury has the unique advantage of having access to 1.4 billion payment records in a given fiscal year. Supervised machine learning could assist human experts in deciding whether to issue a payment based on data and prior history, such as reoccurring benefit payments. Unsupervised learning could help detect fraud by identifying anomalies in the payment data across federal agencies and programs. These models can enable continuous monitoring throughout the payment lifecycle, ensuring swift and adaptive responses to emerging fraud threats.

Advanced analytics can integrate additional data sources and calibrate AI/ML models to meet their unique program requirements. For example, an agency could leverage the location data from a computer or phone being used to apply for federal programs to provide location data or behavioral patterns that help flag potential risk or anomalies. Treasury could become the central hub for reporting suspicious or fraudulent activity in the federal payment lifecycle, as the Department of Homeland Security's Cybersecurity and Infrastructure Security Agency (CISA) does as the operational lead for federal cybersecurity.

Embrace best practices
At the heart of promoting payment integrity is our ability to use data to learn and respond to new and changing requirements, emerging threats, and opportunities to improve the customer experience with digital services.

Payment integrity data catalog and schema. A payment integrity data catalog can support payment decisions by assembling data to be easily identified and integrated into agency pre-award and pre-payment processes. Given the bespoke nature of federal programs, to make centralized data actionable, the data will need to be well documented to include relevant metadata. This payment integrity data catalog should include information including data definitions, authoritative source, formatting, and validation. Moreover, Treasury can expedite the use of authoritative data by mapping the relationships between data and documenting validation rules and logic to enable reuse. Specifically, Treasury can promote connections between payment and award processes by enforcing the use of standard entity identifiers and contract and financial assistance award identifiers in the payment process.

Treasury can build upon the Governmentwide Spending Data Model (GSDM), which powers USAspending.gov and is the authoritative source for the terms, definitions, formats, and structures for hundreds of distinct data elements that show how federal dollars are spent. The benefit of this approach is that the GSDM already makes the fundamental connections between government accounting, budget, procurement, and financial assistance data and is widely adopted by federal agencies to meet federal transparency requirements.[11] Moreover, improper payments reporting requirements established under PIIA and reported in to PaymentAccuracy.gov could be incorporated to improve the connection and alignment with existing federal transparency, financial, and performance reporting, ultimately advancing transparency and accountability to the public.

Secure data sharing. A secure, robust, and scalable computational infrastructure along with well documented Application Program Interfaces (APIs) can streamline access to data and enable data sharing all while protecting privacy and security. For example, the government could address privacy concerns and improve data sharing by establishing "yes"/"no" attribute validation services for key sensitive data such as validating income. Once mature, Congress could point to digital payment integrity validations when developing legislation that establishes new programs or expands existing programs.

The government has already implemented similar services, notably the Social Security Administration's Electronic Consent Based Verification Service (eCBVS) that enables financial institutions to conduct Social Security Number verifications.[12] Similarly, the newly established National Accuracy Clearinghouse (NAC) can help states prevent issuing duplicate Supplemental Nutrition Assistance Program (SNAP) benefits without requiring the storage of personally identifiable information (PII).[13]

Payment monitoring as a service. As with monitoring identity theft using commercial services, the government could empower individuals to monitor payments they receive from the federal government. Today, individuals must go to multiple government agencies to get the status of their benefit payments. Just as government has implemented a centralized platform for vendor invoicing and grant payments,[14] this service could help protect against fraud and identity theft by alerting users of changes to reoccurring payments or new payments. Similarly, with appropriate privacy and security controls in place, federal agencies could subscribe to the service to monitor potentially duplicate or improper payments.

Strengthen partnerships

Strengthening partnerships through collaboration is critical to defending against current payment integrity threats and building toward this future vision. Collaboration and partnerships can reduce startup costs and increase the scale of solutions that reduce improper payments. Three key partnerships will be essential to build and nurture at each level:

Federal agencies and FFSA programs. Given that hundreds of billions of federal funds (over $720 billion annually prior to the COVID-19 pandemic) are administered at the state level, a majority of improper payments are made by programs administered by the state, such as Medicaid or unemployment insurance. Moreover, with federal grants being the fastest growing source of revenue for states, ensuring payment integrity between federal agencies and states is more important than ever.[15] The recently enacted PIIA legislation provides state agencies that manage federally funded state-administered programs, "access to, and use of, the Do Not Pay Initiative for the purpose of verifying payment or award eligibility for payments."[16]

Chief financial officers (CFOs)/financial managers and program managers. One of the biggest disincentives that agencies face in preventing and detecting improper payments and/or fraud is the pressure to get "money out the door" to respond to an emergency and/or to meet statutory requirements. Unfortunately, this can lead to the program office not establishing adequate internal controls up front. At the same time, agency CFOs and financial managers must comply with improper payment reporting requirements but may not have adequate visibility or ability to improve payment integrity. Keeping in mind that financial managers and program managers are ultimately aligned in their desire to execute the agency mission, agencies should promote collaboration and proactive information sharing.

Oversight entities and implementing agencies. Consistent with OMB Memorandum M-22-04, Promoting Accountability through Cooperation among Agencies and Inspectors General (December 3, 2021), collaboration and the sharing of best practices between implementing agencies and the oversight community should be promoted, especially when initiating or significantly expanding new programs.[17] The OMB-led "Gold Standard Meetings" demonstrated that oversight and implementing agencies can promote a cooperative and early prevention model for fraud prevention and program integrity, while still respecting the independence of the oversight community.

In addition to collaboration and information sharing, government needs to gain a deeper understanding of the challenges that stakeholders in the payment lifecycle face to advance payment integrity. Specifically, Treasury can conduct targeted user research to gain a better understanding of current agency and state challenges to detecting and preventing fraud and improper payments. These insights can help Treasury direct its limited resources towards highest value efforts and design payment integrity solutions that integrate with business processes throughout the payment lifecycle.

LOOKING FORWARD

The unprecedented spending in response to the COVID-19 pandemic was a necessary intervention that also exposed federal and state award and payment systems and processes to greater fraud and exacerbated long-standing improper payment challenges. When the need arises to address similar emergencies in the future, the government should be able meet this need without waste, fraud, or abuse.

There is progress being made[18] but more needs to be done. Treasury can play a greater role in promoting payment integrity by empowering federal programs to pursue the vision of detecting and preventing fraud and improper payments in real-time. This vision can be achieved by focusing on prevention through the use of technology and advanced analytics, embracing best practices in data sharing, and strengthening partnerships through collaboration at every level of government. By embracing this vision, the federal government can make significant strides in payment integrity, reduce fraud, and safeguard taxpayer resources.

Renata Miskell is the Deputy Assistant Secretary for Accounting Policy and Financial Transparency, at the U.S. Department of the Treasury, Washington, D.C.

Endnotes

1   S.375—Payment Integrity Information Act of 2019, Public Law 116-117, https://www. congress.gov/bill/116th-congress/senate-bill/375/text.

2   31 U.S.C. 3351(4).

3   U.S. Small Business Administration, "COVID-19 Pandemic EIDL and PPP Loan Fraud Landscape," Report 23-09, June 27, 2023, https://www.sba.gov/document/report-23-09-covid-19-pandemic-eidl-ppp-loan-fraud-landscape.

4   U.S. Government Accountability Office, Improper Payments: Fiscal Year 2022 Estimates and Opportunities for Improvement, GAO-23-106285, March 29, 2023, https://www. gao.gov/products/gao-23-106285.

5   The five program areas include: (1) Medicaid ($81 billion), (2) Medicare ($47 billion), (3) the Paycheck Protection Program ($29 billion), (4) Unemployment Insurance ($19 billion), and (5) Earned Income Tax Credit ($18 billion). See GAO-23-106285.

6   Per OMB, high-priority programs are those programs for which agencies report estimated monetary loss from improper payments in excess of $100 million.

7   See Circular A-123, Appendix C; U.S. Government Accountability Office, Standards for Internal Control in the Federal Government, September 2014, https://www.gao.gov/products/gao-14-704g.

8   U.S. Government Accountability Office, Standards for Internal Control in the Federal Government, September 2014, https://www.gao.gov/products/gao-14-704g.

9   See: U.S. Chief Financial Officers Council and U.S. Treasury, Bureau of the Fiscal
     Service, The Antifraud Playbook, October 2018, https://www.cfo.gov/assets/files/
     Interactive-Treasury-Playbook.pdf; U.S. Government Accountability Office, A Framework
     for Managing Fraud Risks in Federal Programs, July 2015, https://www.gao.gov/assets/
     gao-15-593sp.pdf; and U.S. Government Accountability Office, A Framework for
     Managing Improper Payments in Emergency Assistance Programs, July 2023, https://
     www.gao.gov/assets/gao-23-105876.pdf.

10   U.S. Department of the Treasury, Bureau of the Fiscal Service, Progress Statement 2022:
     The Future of Federal Financial Management, February 2023, https://fmvision.fiscal.trea-
     sury. gov/files/progress-statement-2022.pdf.

11   The Federal Funding Accountability and Transparency Act (FFATA) and the Digital
     Accountability and Transparency (DATA) Act of 2014.

12   U.S. Social Security Administration, "Information About eCBSV," https://www.ssa.gov/
     dataexchange/eCBSV/?tl=0.

13   U.S. Department of Agriculture, Food and Nutrition Service, "National Accuracy Clearing-
     house (NAC)," Updated February 15, 2023, https://www.fns.usda.gov/snap/nac.

14   Invoice Processing Platform (IPP) for vendors and the Automated Standard Application for
     Payments (ASAP) for federal agencies and recipient organizations.

15   GAO, see "Federal Grants to State and Local Governments," https://www.gao.gov/federal-
     grants-state-and-local-governments.

16   S.375—Payment Integrity Information Act of 2019, Public Law 116-117, https://www.
     congress.gov/bill/116th-congress/senate-bill/375/text.

17   Office of Management and Budget Memorandum 22-04, Promoting Accountability
     through Cooperation among Agencies and Inspectors General, December 3, 2021,
     https://www.whitehouse.gov/wp-content/uploads/2021/12/M-22-04-IG-Cooperation.pdf.

18   For example, the GAO, OMB, Treasury, and the Office of Personnel Management (OPM)
     are partnering to advance payment integrity under the Joint Financial Management
     Improvement Program (JFMIP). This effort seeks to strengthen trust in government by
     promoting payment integrity in federal programs, focusing on prevention, promoting best
     practices, and strengthening partnerships.

Chapter Thirteen

Leveraging Inspectors General to Make Evidence-Based Decisions

By Ken Lish
National Science Foundation

INTRODUCTION

The fundamental duties of executives across the federal government are to make informed and timely decisions, and to ensure the effective and efficient delivery of federal programs. Although artificial intelligence (AI) and data analytics receive much fanfare as emerging tools to facilitate effective and evidence-based decisions, an arguably more innovative and meaningful development in this area is taking place in an older and more traditional part of the federal government—the Office of Inspector General (OIG) community.

The role of OIGs has traditionally involved retrospective audits, evaluations, and inspections of agency programs and operations. However, spurred by innovations during the COVID-19 pandemic, the OIG community is embracing a more proactive role to engage with their respective agencies on the design and controls of new programs prior to implementation. By taking a proactive approach and partnering with their OIGs, agency leaders can incorporate data and expertise into their decision making and program development process that is more timely, accurate, and broader.

This approach leads to deeper insights, better informed decisions, improved program delivery, and stronger program integrity. Gene Sperling, White House American Rescue Plan (ARP) coordinator and senior advisor to the Office of the President, in reference to OIG roles during the development of ARP programs, stated: "The oversight community had an enormous amount of expertise. So why would somebody helping to coordinate a major rescue plan only want to read about what they had to say after you had done something wrong? You should be trying to get that expertise early, and if things are going wrong, you want to be the first to know, not the last to know."[1]

This chapter explores the role of an Inspector General (IG), describes agile oversight, and provides examples of how OIGs have used agile oversight in recent years.

Establishing the Role of Inspectors General

The Inspector General Act of 1978, as amended,[2] introduced the concept of OIGs into the civilian side of the federal government. Generally, OIGs are established within agencies with the broad mission of promoting economy and efficiency, and helping to detect and deter fraud, waste, abuse, and mismanagement. Today the OIG community is comprised of more than 14,000 professionals across 74 offices. Through audits, inspections, evaluations, and investigations, these OIGs have enabled significant improvements to government operations, with potential savings in fiscal year 2022 totaling approximately $70.1 billion. With an aggregate FY2022 budget of approximately $3.5 billion across the OIG community, these potential savings represent a $20 return on every dollar invested in OIGs.[3]

Defining Agile Oversight

In response to the COVID-19 pandemic, Congress authorized historic levels of emergency funding totaling more than $5.2 trillion.[4] In addition to the oversight work of individual OIGs, Congress also established the Pandemic Response Accountability Committee (PRAC) to coordinate and support oversight of the emergency funding and the federal government's pandemic response.[5]

Given the magnitude of the funding and the immediate nature of how the funds were issued, OIGs and the PRAC developed a new method of doing business, termed agile oversight. Agile oversight delivers information and insights into the hands of agency decision makers in real-time, saving taxpayer dollars and safeguarding the integrity of government programs. Traditional oversight methods such as audits are retrospective and can take over a year to issue. In an emergency environment where trillions of dollars leave government coffers, real-time insights are critical to ensuring the integrity and effective delivery of government programs.

In response to the broader acceptance and use of agile oversight methods across the OIG community, the PRAC developed the Agile Products Toolkit (Toolkit).[6] The Toolkit aims to aid federal OIGs, state, and local agencies that conduct quick reviews as part of their duties to provide expeditious oversight of federal funds. In defining agile oversight, the Toolkit notes that "agile products can come in many forms depending on agency guidance or expectations."

Primarily, agile products highlight issues requiring immediate action for oversight officials, congressional stakeholders, and others who have requested reviews of high-risk areas. Additionally, agile products can inform affected stakeholders by providing transparency and ensuring that key agency leadership and the public have access to information more quickly.[7] As noted by the U.S. Department of Health and Human Services Inspector General Christi Grimm, "Agile practices maximize timely and relevant oversight" and have "tremendous potential to allow for us to meet the moment."[8]

Promoting Accountability Through Cooperation

One new method of real-time oversight that was developed during the pandemic became known as "Gold Standard" meetings.[9] These meetings brought together officials from the White House, the Office of Management and Budget (OMB), the PRAC, agencies, and their respective OIGs to jointly review new or significantly expanded American Rescue Plan (ARP) programs prior to launch.

The OMB deputy director for management described these meetings as facilitating a way to mitigate risks at the front end of programs with a focus on prevention of fraud and mismanagement: "We want to fully leverage all of the experience and expertise of the oversight community, while respecting its independence. The process has had significant effects on program design and financial controls, leading to more frequent, detailed, and rigorous reporting and continued cooperation and dialogue among agency leaders and their respective agency IGs."[10]

The chair of the PRAC later echoed those comments: "We were doing exactly what the public and the taxpayers would expect of us, which was using our considered, informed knowledge to ensure programs are being run right at the outset, not a year later or two years later."[11]

On December 3, 2021, OMB institutionalized this practice with the issuance of Memorandum M-22-04, Promoting Accountability through Cooperation among Agencies and Inspectors General.[12] In part, this memorandum reestablished the expectation of how agencies should interact with their OIGs. "It is the president's expectation that executive departments and agencies will restore and respect the integrity and independence of their respective agency inspectors general (IGs), and work with the Congress to ensure that IG offices can exercise their vital oversight role."[13]

The memorandum also encouraged agencies to proactively engage with their OIGs to collectively review and assess program design, financial controls, and reporting measures prior to the release of funds from programs that were newly created, received substantial funding increases, or required significant changes to program design. "Collaboration on the frontend ensures expertise is brought to bear to ensure programs are constructed in ways that strike the balance right between efficient results, equitable access, and program integrity, including minimal waste, fraud, and abuse. Agency leaders should replicate this type of front-end collaboration for all significant new programs and existing programs where significant change to program design is being implemented by the agency."[14]

Again, OMB's deputy director for management described the overarching goal of this memorandum as having two major purposes: "One was [to develop] an ongoing expectation for agency leadership on how it is cooperating with their IG on all matters and communicating to their employees that this is base case expectation. And the second, implementing this type of an approach, which is on the front end, it is better for all of us to try and get it right there, than [to] try and pick up the pieces on the back end when something goes wrong."[15]

Agile Oversight in Action

OIGs and agencies across government have built on this approach by implementing agile oversight techniques that facilitate OIGs providing valuable input to agencies during the program development process without jeopardizing their independence. The examples below highlight how OIG's can provide proactive input to international aid responses, identify risks related to newly granted authorities, and provide transparency into risks and spending plans for new programs.

- **Advisory Notice—Key Considerations to Inform USAID's Response in Ukraine,** U.S. Agency for International Development OIG, July 22, 2022.[16] Congress provided the U.S. Agency for International Development (USAID) with $8.5 billion in supplemental appropriations for direct budget support to Ukraine in response to Russia's incursion into the country. By issuing this product, the USAID OIG provided direct and timely insight through highlighting key lessons from prior and relevant oversight work. The USAID OIG identified risks and challenges for the agency's consideration related to procurement, direct cash assistance programs, contributions to World Bank funding mechanisms, sexual exploitation and abuse, program monitoring, and stakeholder coordination. This product provided evidence-based considerations to help agency leadership make more informed decisions and take more effective actions.

- **Summary of Federal OIG Findings and Recommendations Related to Other Transaction Agreements,** National Science Foundation OIG, March 3, 2023.[17] The CHIPS and Science Act of 2022 formally established the U.S. National Science Foundation's (NSF) Technology, Innovation, and Partnerships (TIP) directorate. It also provided NSF with the authority to use other transaction agreements (OTAs) to carry out the activities of the TIP directorate. OTAs are often used to advance new technologies and for research, development, and demonstration projects. Although OTAs are subject to federal fiscal law, they are not subject to other traditional regulations that govern grants, cooperative agreements, and contracts.

As such, agencies must develop rigorous control environments with comprehensive policies, processes, and procedures to ensure proper oversight and accountability over the use of OTAs. NSF's OIG issued this report to inform NSF of potential risks inherent to OTAs as it develops its own OTA policies and procedures. The NSF OIG identified and summarized relevant information from eight reports published by four federal OIGs over the past five years, which contained 19 findings concerning the management of OTAs. In this instance, NSF OIG provided agency leadership with high-quality data and insights that will inform NSF's decisions and help improve programmatic delivery.

- **Flash Report: Orphaned Wells Program,** U.S. Department of the Interior OIG, July 2022.[18] On November 15, 2021, the Infrastructure Investment and Jobs Act (IIJA) was signed into law. The IIJA specifically authorized $4.7 billion in appropriations for the U.S. Department of the Interior (DOI) to administer federal, state, and tribal programs to plug, remediate, and reclaim orphaned gas and oil wells. As documented in the report, orphaned wells pose public health and safety risks as well as environmental risks.

  Further, the cost of plugging a well can be affected by various factors such as depth, condition, location, and accessibility, and can range from $2,400 to $227,000. Additionally, there was a 50 percent increase in the number of documented orphaned wells from 2018 to 2020. Even with the increase in documented orphaned wells, the total number of wells may be significantly higher.

  By issuing this flash report, DOI OIG was able to highlight the uncertainty of the estimates in the underlying programs and to illustrate the challenges that federal and state program administrators will face in plugging, remediating, and reclaiming orphaned wells. The report was also successful in sharing information, promoting transparency to key stakeholders, and identifying how DOI planned to use IIJA funding.

Agile oversight[19] is not a replacement for traditional audits, inspections, evaluations, or investigations. Rather, agile oversight is another tool in an OIG's oversight toolbox. As discussed, this evolution in oversight provides a mechanism for the OIG community to help ensure the effective and efficient delivery of federal programs at the outset. Although it is incumbent upon OIGs to plan and execute their work, agency leadership should feel comfortable approaching their respective OIGs to collaborate on the front-end of significant new initiatives and programs. The trust and confidence needed to create this type of relationship is facilitated by open, constant, and candid communications between agency and OIG personnel.

OMB Memorandum M-22-04 encourages agency leadership and OIGs to "hold routine meetings to have candid discussions in a non-audit setting and maintain clear lines of communication between the appropriate IG officials and agency leadership. Open dialogue allows for discussions on areas that are of most value to the agency and can reduce the risk of antagonism that may otherwise cascade throughout the organization in cases where leadership only engages their IGs when confronted with negative or controversial audit or investigation results."

Although agile oversight products have the potential to add significant value to federal programs, there are inherent risks that must also be managed. Two cornerstones of the effectiveness and overall impact of the OIG community include maintaining independence and strictly adhering to standards of quality control. At the outset of any agile effort, OIGs and agency officials must understand and respect their respective roles and responsibilities. Any collaboration between an agency and its OIG will not result in a seal of approval. Although OIGs may bring to bear their insight and expertise, the responsibility for programmatic and managerial decision making remains the role of agency officials. Failure to define clear roles and responsibilities could result in threats to the OIG's objectivity and independence.

Additionally, OIG products such as audits and evaluations are held to strict quality control standards such as Generally Accepted Government Auditing Standards and the Council of the Inspectors General on Integrity and Efficiency's (CIGIE) Quality Standards for Inspections and Evaluations. However, agile products may not always be compatible with these standards. In such cases, OIGs could elect to follow CIGIE's Quality Standards for Federal Offices of Inspector General, also known as the Silver Book. Regardless of the standard cited, OIGs should indicate that their agile products adhere to professional standards of independence, due professional care, and quality assurance that the engagement team implemented procedures to ensure the accuracy of the information presented.

LOOKING FORWARD

OIGs are well positioned to propel effectiveness in delivering outcomes and optimizing returns on investment while simultaneously maintaining their objectivity and independence. OIG and agency leadership can build trust and strengthen their relationships as a normal course of business. By putting in the hard work during easy times, both parties will be well positioned to collaborate for the benefit of the American taxpayer during the next national emergency or mission expansion.

These strengthened relationships and new approaches to oversight will provide a mechanism for agency leadership to collect more accurate and timely data, conduct more informed analysis, make better decisions, and take smarter actions. By collaborating with OIGs, agency leaders will have access to higher-quality data and insights that can inform decisions and improve programmatic delivery when needed most.

Disclaimer: The views and opinions presented in this chapter do not necessarily represent the views of the NSF OIG or the U.S. government.

Ken Lish *is an Audit Director at the National Science Foundation Office of Inspector General in Alexandria, VA. Ken is responsible for overseeing NSF's programs, operations, and $35 billion grant portfolio.*

Endnotes

1   Keynote Fireside Chat: Lessons in Leadership and Engagement. 2022 CIGIE Leadership Forum. November 16, 2022. Minute 1:48, https://www.youtube.com/watch?v=gX4TXNXkz-Q&list=PLBEthG-7zUGUb-yP8i2FR9jD5Szj3lQrz&index=18.

2   Pub. L. No. 95-452 (Oct. 12, 1978), 5 U.S.C. app. 3.

3   Annual Report to the President and Congress, Fiscal Year 2022. Council of the Inspectors General on Integrity & Efficiency. Pg. I, https://www.ignet.gov/sites/default/files/files/993-043CIGIEAnnualReport2023 _ jm6.pdf.

4   Funding overview. Funding Overview | Pandemic Oversight. Pandemic Response Accountability Committee, https://www.pandemicoversight.gov/data-interactive-tools/funding-overview.

5   PRAC Strategic plan - 2020-2025. Pandemic Response Accountability Committee. Pg. 3, https://www.pandemicoversight.gov/media/file/prac-strategic-plan-july-2020pdf.

6   The Agile Products Toolkit. Pandemic Response Accountability Committee, https://www.pandemicoversight.gov/media/file/agile-products-toolkit2022pdf.

7   The Agile Products Toolkit. Pandemic Response Accountability Committee. Pg. 1. https://www.pandemicoversight.gov/media/file/agile-products-toolkit2022pdf.

8   Inspector General Fireside Chat on Agile Oversight. PRAC Agile Oversight Forum. January 25, 2023. Minute 6:15, https://www.youtube.com/watch?v=3pRknWeRknE&list=PLU-8KdjW9w4N0S2xSKeC9n42o4csfxowe.

9   Keynote Fireside Chat: Lessons in Leadership and Engagement. 2022 CIGIE Lead-
      ership Forum. November 16, 2022. Minute 0:35, https://www.youtube.com/
      watch?v=gX4TXNXkz-Q&list=PLBEthG-7zUGUb-yP8i2FR9jD5Szj3IQrz&index=18.

10   Written Testimony of Jason S. Miller, Deputy Director for Management, Office of Manage-
      ment and Budget. Senate Committee on Homeland Security and Governmental Affairs. Full
      Committee Hearing. Pandemic Response and Accountability: Reducing Fraud and Expand-
      ing Access to COVID-19 Relief Through Effective Oversight. March 17, 2022. Pg. 3, https://
      www.hsgac.senate.gov/wp-content/uploads/imo/media/doc/Testimony-Miller-2022-03-17.
      pdf.

11   Inspector General Fireside Chat on Agile Oversight. PRAC Agile Oversight Forum. January
      25, 2023. Minute 38:53, https://www.youtube.com/watch?v=3pRknWeRknE&list=PLU-
      8KdjW9w4N0S2xSKeC9n42o4csfxowe.

12   Promoting Accountability through Cooperation among Agencies and Inspectors General.
      Office of Management and Budget Memorandum M-22-04. December 3, 2021, https://
      www.whitehouse.gov/wp-content/uploads/2021/12/M-22-04-IG-Cooperation.pdf.

13   Promoting Accountability through Cooperation among Agencies and Inspectors General.
      Office of Management and Budget Memorandum M-22-04. December 3, 2021. Pg. 1,
      https://www.whitehouse.gov/wp-content/uploads/2021/12/M-22-04-IG-Cooperation.pdf.

14   Promoting Accountability through Cooperation among Agencies and Inspectors General.
      Office of Management and Budget Memorandum M-22-04. December 3, 2021. Pg. 4,
      https://www.whitehouse.gov/wp-content/uploads/2021/12/M-22-04-IG-Cooperation.pdf.

15   Keynote Fireside Chat: Lessons in Leadership and Engagement. 2022 CIGIE Lead-
      ership Forum. November 16, 2022. Minute 7:13, https://www.youtube.com/
      watch?v=gX4TXNXkz-Q&list=PLBEthG-7zUGUb-yP8i2FR9jD5Szj3IQrz&index=18.

16   Key Considerations to Inform USAID's Response in Ukraine. U.S. Agency for International
      Development Office of Inspector General. July 22, 2022, https://oig.usaid.gov/sites/
      default/files/2022-07/Ukraine%20Advisory%20-%207 _ 22 _ 2022 _ 0 _ 0.pdf.

17   Summary of Federal OIG Findings and Recommendations Related to Other Transaction
      Agreements. National Science Foundation Office of Inspector General. March 3, 2023,
      https://oig.nsf.gov/sites/default/files/reports/2023-03/23-6-001-Other-Transaction-Agree-
      ments.pdf.

18   Flash Report: Orphaned Wells Program. U.S. Department of the Interior Office of Inspector
      General. July 2022, https://www.doioig.gov/sites/default/files/2021-migration/Flash%20
      Report _ DOI%20OrphanedWells.pdf.

19   Westbrooks, Robert A., *Left Holding the Bag: A Watchdog's Account of How Washington
      Fumbled its COVID Test*, Gracie House LLC, June 14, 2023.

Chapter Fourteen

A "One Agency" Approach to Enhanced Mission Enabling Services

By Jason Briefel
Shaw, Bransford & Roth, P.C.

INTRODUCTION

For over two decades, the federal government has sought to advance shared services policy and business practices within agencies and across the executive branch. Yet limited progress has been made on both fronts because this policy-centric approach skips past the foundations of design, structure, and funding. Agencies should take a step back for a more holistic approach to consider mission enablement functions and their funding. By doing so, agencies can manage these functions through a more rational, transparent, accountable, and consolidated approach, linked to mission outcomes. Once successful at the agency level, the government can enable future broader enterprisewide applications.

This chapter examines NASA's approach to mission enablement services, illustrating a proven example of the "one firm" mindset and approach, and discusses new research findings underscoring the benefits of operating as "one firm."[1] It offers recommendations and considerations for agencies, the Office of Management and Budget, and Congress to move shared services forward in the federal government in a different, and hopefully more successful, way than has been tried over the past two decades.

From Parts to a Whole: A Proven Model for Agency Mission Accomplishment

"Mission support" functions, including financial management (FM), human resources (HR), information technology (IT), procurement, and business support services, have been deemed administrative matters in agencies and are not always positioned as mission-essential. Outside of the IT realm, Congress often lacks visibility into the spending and investments in functions like HR.[2] Congress does not recognize functions like HR as mission-enabling functions that cannot be separated from mission or program delivery, as has been the case in the past.[3]

The current approach devalues, even ignores, mission-enabling functions. In large departments, each bureau or component agency maintains its own FM, HR, IT, and procurement shops. Agencies usually justify this arrangement due to "unique mission requirements." This design is extremely costly and inefficient, and has led to inconsistent results. Further, employees working at bureau-level shops may not necessarily see themselves as departmental employees, and their career opportunities are likely attenuated based on their organization, rather than as part of a broader departmental talent ecosystem. Many of these employees may see their functional mission as their primary responsibility and focus.

The Consolidated Business Services Organization (CBSO) model is a proven model for mission enablement services. It enables a one-agency mindset and operating behaviors, with improved effectiveness, efficiency, and outcomes. With a one-agency mindset, success of the whole is prioritized over any of the individual parts. "Unique mission requirements" cannot continue to be an excuse for programs or agencies persisting with inefficient mission support functions. Government leaders can succeed by focusing on long-term management reforms to drive transformational change that enables a one-agency mindset and yields improved performance.

NASA's Shared Service Center: An Example of Enterprise Mission Enablement Services

NASA's Shared Services Center (NSSC),[4] is a CBSO established in 2006 that operates under a Working Capital Fund.[5] In 2018 the agency realigned mission enabling functions to report centrally, and in 2021 the agency realigned budget from individual Centers to NASA-wide enterprise organizations. Prior to the NSSC, Congress funded each of the 10 NASA space centers and headquarters at differing levels, with different levels of mission support funding. This created "haves" and "have nots" among local mission enabling organizations, and inconsistent results for customers and employees.[6] Imagine potentially receiving 12 different answers to an HR question across the agency, and the frustration, ineffectiveness, risk, and waste associated.

NASA's NSSC has a single mission to achieve operational efficiencies through consolidation, standardization, and automation. Its leaders foster an organizational culture that promotes customer experience, problem solving, collaboration, and responsiveness. Today the NSSC services over 60 business activities in the areas of financial management, human resources, procurement, enterprise services, and agency business support.

Core tenets of NSSC service delivery model include the following:

- Formal governance structure

- Flexible workforce model

- Pricing model and chargeback mechanism

- Structured management of customer interactions

- Transparency in performance, costs, and reporting

- Business intelligence and data-driven decisions

- Innovation and continuous improvement

- Strong central management, through use of service level agreements (SLAs)

The NSSC has proven successful over the past nearly 20 years in achieving five objectives:

1. Improve operations—timeliness, accuracy, consistency of information

2. Normalize service levels agencywide

3. Achieve service excellence

4. Achieve critical mass of "core" expertise

5. Lower costs

Since its opening, the NSSC has met or exceeded over 92 percent of its metrics.

NASA paid off its $42 million investment to stand up the NSSC in four years. NSSC enables cost avoidance of approximately $30 million per year, a figure that steadily increased through the first decade.[7]

Centralizing the management and administration of most mission enablement services within the NSSC enabled NASA to focus more resources and attention on its mission. Using a blended workforce model with both civil servants and contractors, NASA employees can devote more time to strategic activities rather than transactional/administrative tasks, which are handled by contractors. NASA employees realize increased overall satisfaction through efficient, cost-effective delivery of high-quality services.

Top Performing Organizations Operate as 'One Firm'

New research from McKinsey & Company,[8] which "analyzed employee data from 2,000 organizations across 100 countries regarding 37 discrete management practices and nine effectiveness outcomes," identifies significant organizational performance benefits from operating as 'one firm.'

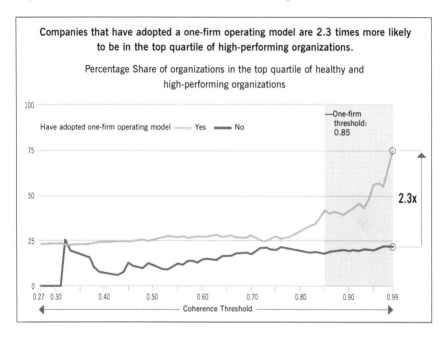

Many large organizations tend to operate in siloed manners, fostering an 'us versus them' mindset among divisions and staff. Executives have been incentivized to optimize their P&L and grow their own domain, with significant implications for organizational culture, expected behaviors, and company performance. Government leaders can learn from organizations—such as Ford, Microsoft, and IBM—which have transitioned successfully to a 'one firm' mindset and operating posture, shifting incentives, behavior, and culture.

The McKinsey report recommends putting "a purposefully interdependent organization structure in place," and then reinforcing this with formal mechanisms. To do so, leadership should align the organization's mission against at least three co-equal axes[9] that serve to integrate siloed interests across the organization and optimize the whole over any part:[10]

1. Accountability for integrating clients/customers

2. Building products and capabilities

3. Optimizing shared services and business enablement

The NSSC offers a clear example of these principles being operationalized in government and yielding positive results.

One-firm targets and incentives require organizations to redefine and elevate their financial management and human resources roles. The one-firm vision requires FM functions to transition from a compliance-oriented mindset towards a forward-leaning, anticipatory, and advisory posture. Rather than focusing on balance sheets as the basis of accountability, FM insights should inform peer-led accountability in service of the entire firm's mission success. Similarly, HR functions must focus on reinforcing incentives and behaviors that drive the one-firm mindset. Core to this is a focus on talent development across and through the organization's talent ecosystem and "ensuring that the behavioral aspects of target setting and evaluation are well calibrated and consistent across" the organization.

Too often in government, local organizational equities are prioritized over broader organizational effectiveness and cultivation of an improvement-oriented mindset. The NSSC has made notable progress in overcoming these barriers. More than 75 percent of fortune 500 companies use a shared service model to improve service and cost savings.[11] NASA's journey reflects the challenges and realities of overcoming entrenched cultural and behavioral norms, and the limits of efficiencies alone to drive change in government absent a hard financial bottom line.

Finally, agencies should invest time in bringing people together from different parts of the organization to socialize, build connections, and enhance appreciation that reinforce commitments to a one-firm mindset aligned with an agency's core mission.[12]

Beyond Budget: Making the Change Happen

As missions continue to expand, most federal agencies are not getting more resources in a post-COVID-19 era. Agencies cannot expect significant infusions of new resources for their mission enablement functions outside IT and cyber. This is especially true when many agencies cannot properly account for the costs, effectiveness, and efficiency of their mission enablement functions, and when the government presently lacks a mechanism to compare the relative performance and costs of these functions across agencies and against industry benchmarks.

There is a checkered history of federal agencies seeking to operate better as "one agency." For example, almost every secretary of the Department of Homeland Security (DHS) has sought to promote a "One DHS" culture and business practice.[13] For 20 years, these efforts have had one key ingredient: leadership focus. But this quickly became the *only* ingredient. Every other aspect of DHS—from its compilation of previously-independent components to its scattered congressional oversight and appropriations authorities–was entirely disparate.[14] Absent close coordination and cooperation with Congress to understand how DHS and its components could more rationally fund and operate their mission enabling functions, DHS central management efforts have been unable to overcome the inertia of bureau and programmatic operations. Without incentives and benefits for leaders and component organizations to embrace "One DHS" coming from Congress, leadership from the top could only go so far.

During the Trump administration, there was an explicit focus on agency mission enablement services as part of its President's Management Agenda PMA.[15] GSA and OMB led a multiyear benchmarking initiative of CFO Act agencies and published data[16] about the quality of services and support that agencies receive in the domains of HCM, FM, IT, and procurement. This data was used to drive discussions among the President's Management Council, as well as the functional C-Suite Councils for leaders in HR, FM, IT, and procurement, and offered a level of transparency such that agency and administration officials could see relative performance and results. The Biden administration's PMA does not address shared service in any specific way. Goal 3 does focus on improvements to financial management, grants, and procurement as core to "the business of government."

Two decades of a White House-driven, waterfall approach to expanding shared services at the agency level and across the federal enterprise has not moved the needle. Instead, agencies should first look inward through a one-firm mindset and design lens to consolidate and rationalize their mission enabling functions into a CBSO, following the NASA model. Doing so will enhance the capability and quality of those functions, reduce costs, and offer new opportunities for employees to grow professionally.

Minute focus on discrete parts and programs of agencies has obscured the more important bigger picture, perpetuated inefficiencies, and reinforced siloed behaviors and culture. Little focus has been given to how an entire agency is working. The one-firm model and mindset presents an alternative lens for agency leaders, the White House, and Congress to consider how agencies are structured, funded, enabled, and nudged to achieve their missions better through shared services.

LOOKING FORWARD

Recommendations and Insights

Leaders can focus on cultivating certain skills to enable a one-firm mindset and culture. Change is a difficult process, especially when both individuals and organizations are asked to shift their behaviors and mindsets. To be successful, leaders should identify small wins to see how these contribute toward a greater whole. Celebrating these stories reinforces behaviors to build confidence in the workforce and promote benefits across the enterprise.

Fostering organizations focused on learning and growth comes next, along with a recommendation to "invest in equipping colleagues to work through conflict constructively." While advances in shared services across an agency may not always be successful, the answer to failures should not be "this won't work" but rather should reflect lessons for "how it can work better next time."

The NSSC and the 'one firm' mindset offer important lessons and pose questions for lawmakers, the administration, and agency leaders.

Recommendations for Agencies

- Ensure alignment between the right level of funding of mission enabling services to overall agency budget for mission execution.

- Ensure the agency has the right metrics with supporting data to track mission enabling functions performance, benchmarked against best in class (internal and external to government).

- Research the opportunity for cost savings and improved services within an agency by using common mission-enabling functions centrally managed or through shared service providers.

- Explore the feasibility and potential benefits of establishing a CBSO within the agency.

- Ensure leadership visibility for primary mission support systems in FM, HR, IT, acquisition, and grants identifying the following:
  - Year of initial implementation

  - Estimated year of end of life

  - Annual cost of operating, including all associated IT and labor costs

  - Total cost of ownership from beginning to end

Assessment Questions

- How is leadership, from the agency head, through the career SES and down, working to align budget, culture, incentives, and behavior towards achieving the agency's mission and goals?

- How much is spent providing mission-enablement functions including FM, HR, IT, Procurement, facilities, etc. within components and across the entire organization?

- Has GAO or the agency IG identified management challenges or mission risks related to mission enablement functions? What are the broader lessons for the agency from these cumulative reports, when read through a one-firm mindset?

Recommendations for OMB

- Reboot the mission enablement services benchmark and customer satisfaction initiatives and expand to all agencies.

- Establish a cadre of crosscutting analysts for mission enabling services across the federal government.

- Articulate how budget offices track mission support funding and their linkages to mission outcomes and performance.

- Identify shared services ripe for enterprisewide adoption.

- Identify commodity transactional services that industry may be best positioned to deliver.

- Develop a framework and criteria to assist agencies and Congress in advancing appropriate consolidation of mission enabling functions—and other common functions—at the agency-level and at the government-wide level.

- Clarify where shared services fit within the President's Management Agenda

Assessment Questions

- How could improving the effectiveness and efficiency of mission-enablement services be made part of the President's Management Agenda, and could the one-firm mindset fit into Priority Goal 3 Managing the Business of Government?[17]

- How might competition be fostered within the CXO Councils to identify and promote service excellence and increase adoption of improved practices within discrete management functions and within agencies?

Recommendations for Congress

- Assess the extent of duplication and redundancy in mission support services that exists at the "corporate" and "operating unit" levels throughout departments or agencies.

- Strengthen oversight focus on agency management challenges, as well as the President's Management Agenda.

- Push agency heads for answers about the costs and effectiveness of their mission-enabling services, and their plans to modernize them.

- Understand limitations or constraints that could enable agencies to operate more rationally and better with less funding. Ask what functions could or should be consolidated to the agency level, or more broadly to the federal enterprise level.

- Ask agencies if they have considered eliminating duplicative services by consolidating them internally into a shared service within the agency.

- Adopt lessons from the FITARA Scorecard that could inform a diagnostic for all agency mission enablement functions, to be used in oversight and agency funding decisions.

- Resolve multi-committee jurisdiction oversight issues, exemplified by DHS.

The NASA example demonstrates the potential and real benefits to federal agencies from consolidating mission enablement functions. The one-firm organizations identified in the McKinsey study referenced in this chapter illustrate what can be done by government agencies in adopting a one-firm mindset, culture, and operating model. The recommendations and questions outlined above can help government agency leaders chart a path forward.

Jason Briefel is a Partner and Director of Government & Public Affairs at Shaw, Bransford & Roth, P.C., in Washington, D.C.

Endnotes

1   "One firm means hearing "we, us, and our" language versus "me, mine, and theirs." It means there is one brand identity and a "firm way" of doing things," according to a new McKinsey Company paper discussed in this article.

2   Congress has deemed IT as worthy of regular oversight, investment tracking, and spending review. For example, Congress passed Clinger-Cohen Act of 1996 and Federal Information Technology Acquisition Reform Act (FITARA).

3   Friedman, Drew. "Over Half of GAO's High-Risk Areas Stem from Critical Skills Gaps." *Federal News Network*, April 27, 2023, https://federalnewsnetwork.com/agency-oversight/2023/04/over-half-of-gaos-high-risk-areas-stem-from-critical-skills-gaps/.

4   "Historical Timeline A Look to the Past—Focused on Improving the Future," NASA Shared Services Center, Accessed August 2, 2023, https://searchpub.nssc.nasa.gov/servlet/sm.web.Fetch/NSSC_History_Timeline_for_Web.pdf?rhid=1000&did=586614&type=released.

5   NASA WCF, authorized by Congress in 2003, is a type of revolving fund used to promote total cost visibility and full cost recovery of support services, with a goal to break-even. Efficiency-driven savings are reinvested in the NSSC's ongoing modernization efforts, and can also be applied to the mission directly. Contractor support to the NSSC enables ongoing investments in modern technology capabilities.

6   Wilkers, Ross. "NASA sets example for making shared services work," *Washington Technology*, May 18, 2017, https://washingtontechnology.com/2017/05/nasa-sets-example-for-making-shared-services-work/343739/.

7   Center for Organizational Excellence. "Create Mission Strength Through Shared Services: Improving government service and saving taxpayer money." April 2023.

8   Epstein, Blair, Caitlin Hewes, and Scott Keller. "Capturing the value of 'one firm,'" *McKinsey Quarterly*, May 9, 2023, https://www.mckinsey.com/capabilities/strategy-and-corporate-finance/our-insights/capturing-the-value-of-one-firm.

9   "It is hard to break down organizational silos if the organization is designed around them. Most firms have a dominant organizing axis, be it product, geography, function, or client segment. Results are driven by the sum of P&Ls from the dominant axis. To become a one-firm firm, a shift needs to be made so that no axis matters more than another; instead, each axis should have a clearly defined yet interdependent role in delivering the P&L of the whole firm."

10 "Client/customer integrators have nothing to take to market without the product and capability developers, and product and capability developers cannot get to market without going through the client/customer integrators. Both client/customer integrators and product and capability developers will draw on the shared-services and business-enablement functions, whose mandate is to support them. Ultimately, in a one-firm firm, the individual mandate of all three becomes subservient to the collective mandate to optimize for the whole versus maximizing for any individual part."

11 Center for Organizational Excellence. "Create Mission Strength Through Shared Services: Improving government service and saving taxpayer money." April 2023.

12 Researcher Michael Arena has also highlighted the importance of social networks and connections for organizational culture and performance.

13 Painter, William. "DHS Unity of Effort: Homeland Security Issues in the 116th Congress." Congressional Research Service, March 8, 2019, https://www.everycrsreport.com/files/20190308_IN11069_c5c5043e5281fc0065b651d59b6e56a9afab6c8d.pdf

14 Welder, Scott, Christine Kwon, and Jennifer Dresden. "There's just one Department of Homeland Security. So why does it have so many bosses in Congress?" *The Washington Post*, October 21, 2021, https://www.washingtonpost.com/politics/2021/10/21/theres-just-one-department-homeland-security-so-why-does-it-have-so-many-bosses-congress/.

15 United States. Office of Management and Budget. "M-19-16: Centralized Mission Support Capabilities for the Federal Government." [Washington, D.C.] :Executive Office of the President, Office of Management and Budget, April 26, 2019, https://www.whitehouse.gov/wp-content/uploads/2019/04/M-19-16.pdf.

16 United States. Performance.Gov. "Sharing Quality Services: Improving Efficiency and Effectiveness of Mission Support Services Across Government." [Washington, D.C.], December 2020, https://assets.performance.gov/archives/action_plans/jan_2021_Sharing_Quality_Services.pdf.

17 United States. Performance.Gov. "PMA Priority Goal 3: Managing the Business of Government." [Washington, D.C.], May 2023, https://www.performance.gov/pma/businessofgov/.

Chapter Fifteen

Building and Maintaining Customer Trust in Government Services

By Michael Windle and
Heath Mitchell, FEMA

INTRODUCTION

In the Gettysburg Address, President Abraham Lincoln made famous the reference to "government of the people, by the people, for the people." He did so at the height of the Civil War, a time when belief in the United States was fractured almost to the point of no return. While the nation has come a long way since 1863, the faith Americans have in the federal government is at a new sustained low. According to the Pew Foundation, which has tracked trust in social institutions since the 1950s, for the last 20 years, less than one-third of Americans trust in the federal government.[1]

Declining trust in government is not purely an American phenomenon. The UN's Decade of Action[2] and the OECD's Reinforcing Democracy Initiative[3] are both efforts to improve trust in well-established national governments, parliaments, and democratic systems. In America, the federal government's answer has been a sustained and deliberate recommitment to work "for the people." Across administrations, parties, and generations, government leaders have been working to improve the delivery of government services for the benefit of everyday Americans, with specific attention being paid to the metric of trust in the federal government. Over the presidencies of Biden,[4,5,6] Trump,[7] Obama,[8,9,10] Bush,[11] and Clinton,[12,13] an always similar, sometimes rebranded effort has existed to improve trust in the federal government under banners such as customer service, electronic government, digital government, service delivery, and customer experience (CX).

This chapter will describe how the ongoing evolution of the U.S. federal government customer experience efforts can ultimately succeed. It will also make a series of predictions on areas where government customer experience will face the biggest challenges for the next few decades.

Successful Trajectory of Current Efforts

Perhaps rather optimistically viewed, current government CX efforts can find success due to four primary reasons:

- An ever-improving set of **minimum CX requirements and activities** for federal agencies

- A **growing workforce** of CX-minded and tech-savvy federal employees

- The **institutionalization** of the federal CX movement within individual departments and agencies

- An active **ecosystem** of vendors, advocates, and Congress to continue pushing federal CX forward from all directions

The federal government emphasis to create minimum CX standards and activities across agencies has historically focused on a manageable number of agencies that represent the public's most important interactions with government. In 2016, an Office of Management and Budget (OMB) memo[14] identified these as 28 Core Federal Services.[15] And now in 2023, OMB recognizes 35 High Impact Service Providers.[16,17] Across administrations, this group of federal programs has been the target for coaching, staff, funding, reporting, and leadership attention. The expectations of these programs will continue to grow over time, along with the baseline level of customer experience capabilities and requirements.

Improving the federal customer experience requires a well-trained workforce that knows how to use and apply service design principles, customer feedback, and technology capabilities that improve interactions and touchpoints with customers. The growing talent pipeline for this work now includes a number of specialized hiring programs and offices: Presidential Innovation Fellows (August 2012),[18] 18F (March 2014),[19] the U.S. Digital Service (August 2014),[20] the Subject Matter Expert Qualification Assessments (SME-QA) hiring process (January 2019),[21] and the U.S. Digital Corps (August 2021).[22] Across these programs, goals include bringing a new skillset into the workforce, changing agency cultures, and facilitating a service mindset focused on ownership of the customer experience.

Within those agencies, CX institutionalization will continue, driven both by requirements from Congress as well as agency and department leadership. This institutionalization has come in the form of various advocate or ombuds person offices to resolve specific issues brought to them by customers, as well as divisions, directorates, or bureaus created to proactively improve the customer experience. To date, institutionalization has included actions by Congress (see Figure 1), as well as the creation of customer experience offices by department or agency leadership (see Figure 2)—all of which improves momentum and continuity across administrations.

Figure 1. CX Institutionalization by Congress

1976	Congress creates the Office of Advocacy within the U.S. Small Business Administration[23]
1988	Congress codifies the Office of the Taxpayer Ombudsman within the IRS[24]
1996	Congress replaces the IRS's Office of the Taxpayer Ombudsman with the Office of the Taxpayer Advocate[25]
2003	Congress creates the Medicare Beneficiary Ombudsman within CMS[26]
2008	Congress creates the Office of the Ombudsman within the Federal Housing Finance Agency[27]
2010	Congress creates the Consumer Financial Protection Bureau[28]
2014	Congress creates a Flood Insurance Advocate for FEMA's National Flood Insurance Program[29]

Figure 2. CX Institutionalization by departments or agencies

2010	Department of Education establishes the Chief Customer Experience Officer for Federal Student Aid[30]
2012	Export–Import Bank of the United States hires a Chief Customer Officer[31]
2014	General Services Administration hires a Chief Customer Officer[32,33,34]
2014	Department of Veterans Affairs hires a Chief Customer Service Officer and establishes a Veterans Experience Office[35,36,37]
2020	Office of Customer Experience within the Department of Agriculture[38]
2023	Customer Experience Directorate within the Department of Homeland Security[39]

Lastly, a growing and active ecosystem of vendors and advocacy groups—with influence extending into state and local government service delivery—continues to push federal CX efforts forward from all directions. This "civic tech" ecosystem includes nonprofits, private companies, and advocacy groups such as Code for America and its Safety Net Innovation Lab,[40] Nava,[41] U.S. Digital Response,[42] Bloom Works,[43] and others. When combined, these factors—minimum CX standards, a growing talent pipeline, institutionalization, and an active ecosystem—can make current federal CX efforts successful, but also reveal a set of new challenges on the horizon.

Emerging Challenges and Areas of Focus

In the future, the most significant challenges related to federal customer experience will emerge where public goods and services intersect with private goods and services—for instance, when private companies deliver public goods, or with customer journeys that require both government and private sector transactions. As examples of the challenges when private companies execute public goods, look no further than government funded loans and insurance,[44] commitments to privacy, and follow through on the 21st Century IDEA Act.

In these situations, the following challenges will emerge and become problematic as federal CX continues to mature:

- Competition over **ownership of the relationship** with the customer when the ultimate good or service provided is supplied and financed by the government

- New challenges in **maintaining customer privacy**

- The federal government's **difficulty keeping pace** with changing consumer preferences and private sector capabilities

Private firms who develop their competitive advantage by providing a good customer experience may be unwilling to share data, insights, processes, and information that would help other providers and overseeing government agencies to improve their customer experience. Without access to these insights, government may find it harder to exercise authority over improving the customer journeys that it administers. This can also lead to a kind of "provider displacement," where a private partner supersedes government as the service provider in the public imagination. For example, in the case of student loans and crop insurance, the Department of Education[45,46] and Department of Agriculture[47] (respectively) underwrite and finance a product that students and farmers see as being provided by the bank or insurance company of their choice. The extent to which Americans mistake public services for private transactions would limit attempts to improve trust in government institutions. The federal government must take care when relying on private partners for service delivery to ensure that such partnerships properly allocate responsibilities and ownership. Without special attention the federal government may inadvertently limit opportunities to participate in human-centered design processes.

As government customer experience efforts mature, they face growing challenges to keep up with changing customer expectations influenced by new technology and private sector offerings. For example, in 2010 the Transportation Security Administration (TSA) began pushing boundaries of government data collection with body scan technology at airport security checkpoints.[48,49] Within a year, a biometric security services company called CLEAR was founded[50] and began exploring contract opportunities with TSA. The quickly established technology gap between the TSA and its private partner, which uses retinal and digital fingerprint scanning tools to whitelist entrants, exemplifies the challenges government will continue to face in catching up with technology modernization.

Outdated laws can undermine government's ability to deliver high quality experiences. For example, the Privacy Act of 1974 is nearly 50 years old and has not kept up as individuals' privacy expectations have changed. Advances in technology, relational databases, and computer matching were beyond the realm of possibility when the legislation was initially drafted. Timely implementation of new laws is another area that illustrates the challenge government has when trying to keep pace with technological change. For example, though the 21st Century IDEA Act was signed into law in late 2018, many legislative goals have not been met and federal agencies still have a long way to go to effectively implement this law.[51,52]

Not all government efforts need to be inflexible or slow. A more flexible, scalable, and effective model for government transformation exists in the biannual FITARA scorecards initially implemented in 2015. Now in their fourteenth iteration, these scorecards leverage changing categories and standards that are updated with each edition, improving the government's ability to "keep up" with changing expectations and technologies.[53] To succeed in improving the customer experience, the federal government must develop new ways to meet the public's technology expectations even as private sector tech champions move forward.

LOOKING FORWARD

The increasing lack of trust in government cannot be ignored. With ongoing commitment, efforts already in place to improve federal customer experience capabilities can succeed. Agencies are restoring trust in government by incrementally rebuilding trust in individual government services. Improved CX requirements for federal agencies, alongside a growing workforce of CX-minded and tech-savvy federal employees, can galvanize the institutionalization of CX best practices across the federal government. The existing principles that underpin customer experience and human-centered design are essential tools to restoring trust in government.

Policymakers and other government leaders must also look towards the new challenges that will occur with the further blending of public and private goods. Public entities must continue to lead in the customer journeys they are responsible for, regardless of who executes the transaction or service. For goods and services primarily provided by government agencies, as well as those provided through public-private partnerships, agencies must continue to progress beyond understanding their customers to ensure that government programs continue to earn back customer trust.

Michael Windle *leads marketing efforts for FEMA's National Flood Insurance Program. He previously served as CX Team Lead in FEMA's Individual Assistance Division, and also worked at OMB leading the Recovering from a Disaster Life Experience effort created by Executive Order 14058. In 2020, Michael founded FEMA's Grassroots Customer Experience Community.*

Heath Mitchell *supports front office operations for FEMA's Federal Insurance Directorate in Washington, D.C., where he coordinates activities for the High Impact Service: filing a claim under the National Flood Insurance Program. Heath Co-Chairs FEMA's Grassroots Customer Experience Community, which advocates for more FEMA services to embrace principles of human-centered design.*

Disclaimer: The views and opinions presented in this chapter do not represent the views of FEMA or the U.S. federal government.

Endnotes

1   Pew Research Center, June 2022, Americans' Views of Government: Decades of Distrust, Enduring Support for Its Role. https://www.pewresearch.org/politics/2022/06/06/americans-views-of-government-decades-of-distrust-enduring-support-for-its-role/.

2   Perry, Jonathan. Trust in public institutions: Trends and implications for economic security. United Nations Department of Economic and Social Affairs, Policy Brief 108, June 2021. https://www.un.org/development/desa/dspd/wp-content/uploads/sites/22/2021/08/PB_108.pdf.

3   "OECD Reinforcing Democracy Initiative," Organisation for Economic Co-operation and Development, July 1, 2023. https://www.oecd.org/governance/reinforcing-democracy/.

4   U.S. President, Executive Order, "Advancing Racial Equity and Support for Underserved Communities Through the Federal Government, Executive Order 13985 of January 20, 2021," Federal Register 86, no. 14 (January 25, 2021): 7009, https://www.federalregister.gov/documents/2021/01/25/2021-01753/advancing-racial-equity-and-support-for-underserved-communities-through-the-federal-government.

5   U.S. President, Executive Order, "Transforming Federal Customer Experience and Service Delivery To Rebuild Trust in Government, Executive Order 14058 of December 13, 2021," Federal Register 86, no. 239 (December 16, 2021): 71357, https://www.federalregister.gov/documents/2021/12/16/2021-27380/transforming-federal-customer-experience-and-service-delivery-to-rebuild-trust-in-government.

6   Executive Office of the President, President's Management Agenda: Priority 2 Delivering Excellent, Equitable, and Secure Federal Services and Customer Experience (Washington, D.C.: 2021), https://www.performance.gov/pma/.

7   Executive Office of the President, President's Management Agenda: CAP Goal 4 Improving Customer Experience With Federal Services (Washington, D.C.: 2018), https://trumpwhitehouse.archives.gov/wp-content/uploads/2018/04/ThePresidentsManagementAgenda.pdf.

8   U.S. President, Executive Order, "Streamlining Service Delivery and Improving Customer Service, Executive Order 13571 of April 27, 2011," Federal Register 76, no. 84 (May 2, 2011): 24339, https://www.federalregister.gov/documents/2011/05/02/2011-10732/streamlining-service-delivery-and-improving-customer-service.

9   U.S. President, Executive Order, "Using Behavioral Science Insights To Better Serve the American People, Executive Order 13707 of September 15, 2015," Federal Register 80, no. 181 (September 18, 2015): 56365, https://www.federalregister.gov/documents/2015/09/18/2015-23630/using-behavioral-science-insights-to-better-serve-the-american-people.

10 Office of Management and Budget, M-16-08 Memorandum for the Heads of Executive Departments and Agencies: Establishment of the Core Federal Services Council, by Shaun Donovan, (Washington, D.C., 2016), https://obamawhitehouse.archives.gov/sites/default/files/omb/memoranda/2016/m-16-08.pdf.

11 Executive Office of the President, President's Management Agenda: Government-wide Initiative 4 Expanded Electronic Government (Washington, D.C.: 2002), https://obamawhitehouse.archives.gov/sites/default/files/omb/assets/omb/budget/fy2002/mgmt.pdf.

12 Executive Office of the President, Vice President Al Gore's National Performance Review: 1994 Report: Putting Customers First: Standards for Serving the American People (Washington, D.C., 1994), https://govinfo.library.unt.edu/npr/library/nprrpt/csrpt/cusfir94/267e.html

13 U.S. President, Executive Order, "Setting Customer Service Standards, Executive Order 12862 of September 11, 1993," Federal Register 58, no. 176 (September 14, 1993), https://www.archives.gov/files/federal-register/executive-orders/pdf/12862.pdf.

14 Office of Management and Budget, M-16-08 Memorandum for the Heads of Executive Departments and Agencies: Establishment of the Core Federal Services Council, by Shaun Donovan, (Washington, D.C., 2016), https://obamawhitehouse.archives.gov/sites/default/files/omb/memoranda/2016/m-16-08.pdf.

15 Core Federal Services were defined to be "high-volume, high-impact Federal programs that provide transactional services directly to the public."

16 Executive Office of the President, President's Management Agenda: Priority 2, Strategy 1 (Washington, D.C., 2021), https://www.performance.gov/pma/vision/.

17 Executive Office of the President, Designated High Impact Service Providers 2021 (Washington, D.C., 2021), https://www.performance.gov/cx/assets/files/HISP-listing-2021.pdf.

18 The White House, Office of the Press Secretary, White House Launches Presidential Innovation Fellows Program (Washington, D.C., 2012), https://obamawhitehouse.archives.gov/the-press-office/2012/08/23/white-house-launches-presidential-innovation-fellows-program.

19 General Services Administration, Technology Transformation Services, TTS mission, history, and values (Washington, D.C., 2023), https://handbook.tts.gsa.gov/about-us/tts-history/.

20 Executive Office of the President, Office of Management and Budget, U.S. Digital Service, Our Mission (Washington, D.C., 2023), https://www.usds.gov/mission.

21 Executive Office of the President, Office of Management and Budget, U.S. Digital Service, Changing how the government hires technical talent (Washington, D.C., 2023), https://www.usds.gov/projects/smeqa.

22 General Services Administration, Technology Transformation Services, United States Digital Corps, Who We Are (Washington, D.C., 2023), https://digitalcorps.gsa.gov/about/.

23 U.S. Small Business Administration, Office of Advocacy, About (Washington, D.C., 2023), https://advocacy.sba.gov/about/.

24 U.S. Department of the Treasury, Internal Revenue Service, Taxpayer Advocate Service, Our History, (Washington, D.C., 2023), https://www.taxpayeradvocate.irs.gov/about-us/our-history/.

25 U.S. Department of the Treasury, Internal Revenue Service, Taxpayer Advocate Service, Our History, (Washington, D.C., 2023), https://www.taxpayeradvocate.irs.gov/about-us/our-history/.

26 U.S. Department of Health and Human Services, Centers for Medicare & Medicaid Service, Medicare Beneficiary Ombudsman, (Washington, D.C., 2023), https://www.cms.gov/Center/Special-Topic/Ombudsman/Medicare-Beneficiary-Ombudsman-Home.

27 Federal Housing Finance Agency, Ombudsman (Washington, D.C., 2023), https://www.fhfa.gov/AboutUs/Pages/About-The-Ombudsman.aspx.

28 Consumer Financial Protection Bureau, About Us, (Washington, D.C., 2023), https://www.consumerfinance.gov/about-us/.

29 U.S. Congress, Homeowner Flood Insurance Affordability Act of 2014: Public Law 113-89 (Washington, D.C., 2014), https://www.congress.gov/113/plaws/publ89/PLAW-113publ89.pdf.

30 Wensil, Brenda, "StudentAid.gov's 1st Year: What We've Learned and Where We're Going." Digital.gov, September 13, 2013. https://digital.gov/2013/09/13/studentaid-govs-1st-year-what-weve-learned-and-where-were-going/.

31 Thum, Stephanie, "Will 2016 Be the Federal Government's 'Year of the Customer?'" Digital.gov, December 1, 2014. https://digital.gov/2014/12/01/will-2016-be-the-federal-governments-year-of-the-customer/.

32 Chrousos, Phaedra, "Walking in Our Customers' Shoes." Digital.gov, January 16, 2015, https://digital.gov/2015/01/16/walking-in-our-customers-shoes/.

33 Shueh, Jason, "GSA Innovates Services with Chief Customer Officer." Government Technology, March 31, 2015, https://www.govtech.com/workforce/gsa-innovates-services-with-chief-customer-officer.html.

34 Rose, Francis, "GSA's Chrousos: Digital services shifting mindsets to Internet 2.0." Federal News Network. October 8, 2015, https://federalnewsnetwork.com/all-news/2015/10/gsas-chrousos-digital-services-shifting-mindsets-internet-2-0/.

35 Trumbell, Mark, "Why 'chief customer-service officer' could hold key to Veterans Affairs reset." Christian Science Monitor. November 10, 2014, https://www.csmonitor.com/USA/Military/2014/1110/Why-chief-customer-service-officer-could-hold-key-to-Veterans-Affairs-reset.

36 U.S. Department of Veteran Affairs, Veterans Affairs Secretary McDonald Updates Employees on MyVA Reorganization Plans (Washington, D.C., 2014), https://news.va.gov/press-room/veterans-affairs-secretary-mcdonald-updates-employees-on-myva-reorganization-plans/.

37 U.S. Department of Veteran Affairs, Veterans Experience Office, (Washington, D.C., 2023), https://department.va.gov/administrations-and-offices/veterans-experience-office/.

38 U.S. Department of Agriculture, Office of Customer Experience (OCX), (Washington, D.C., 2023), https://www.usda.gov/da/ocx.

39 Doubleday, Justin, "DHS Launching New 'customer Experience' Directorate This Month," *Federal News Network*, June 20, 2023, https://federalnewsnetwork.com/management/2023/06/dhs-launching-new-customer-experience-directorate-this-month/.

40 Code for America. "Code for America Unveils First Cohort of State Partners to Launch Effort Transforming Nation's Social Safety Net." May 18, 2022, https://codeforamerica.org/news/first-state-cohort-safety-net-innovation-lab/.

41 Nava. "Impact." Accessed July 1, 2023, https://www.navapbc.com/impact.

42 U.S. Digital Response. "About." Accessed July 1, 2023, https://www.usdigitalresponse.org/about.

43 Bloomworks. "About." Accessed July 1, 2023, https://bloomworks.digital/mission/.

44 Examples include small business loans and student loans financed by the Small Business Administration or Department of Education, but executed and serviced by banks, as well as crop insurance and flood insurance financed by the Department of Agriculture and Federal Emergency Management Agency, but executed and serviced by private insurance companies.

45 Cordray, Richard, "Announcing the Next Generation of Federal Student Loan Servicing." *Home Room*, May 19, 2022, https://blog.ed.gov/2022/05/announcing-the-next-generation-of-federal-student-loan-servicing/.

46 U.S. Department of Education, "U.S. Department of Education's Office of Federal Student Aid Awards New Contracts to Five Companies to Serve Borrowers, Reduce Delinquency, and Improve Accountability." (Washington, D.C., 2023), https://www.ed.gov/news/press-releases/us-department-educations-office-federal-student-aid-awards-new-contracts-five-companies-serve-borrowers-reduce-delinquency-and-improve-accountability.

47 U.S. Department of Agriculture, "About the Risk Management Agency." (Washington, D.C., 2021), https://www.rma.usda.gov/en/Fact-Sheets/National-Fact-Sheets/About-the-Risk-Management-Agency.

48 Congressional Research Service, "Airport Body Scanners: The Role of Advanced Imaging Technology in Airline Passenger Screening," September 20, 2012, https://crsreports.congress.gov/product/pdf/R/R42750.

49 Berti, Adele, "Timeline: The History of Airport Body Scanners," *Airport Technology*, April 6, 2020, https://airport.nridigital.com/air_mar20/timeline_the_history_of_airport_body_scanners.

50 Crunchbase. "Clear." Accessed July 1, 2023, https://www.crunchbase.com/organization/clearme.

51 Office of Management and Budget, M-23-22 Memorandum for the Heads of Executive Departments and Agencies: Delivering a Digital First Public Experience, by Shalanda D. Young (Washington, DC, 2023). https://www.whitehouse.gov/wp-content/uploads/2023/09/M-23-22-Delivering-a-Digital-First-Public-Experience.pdf.

52 Miller, Jason, "OMB gives agencies a 10-year digital services transformation framework." *Federal News Network*. September 22, 2023, https://federalnewsnetwork.com/it-modernization/2023/09/omb-gives-agencies-a-10-year-digital-services-transformation-framework/.

53 U.S. Government Accountability Office, Information Technology: Biannual Scorecards Have Evolved and Served as Effective Oversight Tools, GAO 22-105659 (Washington, D.C., 2022), https://www.gao.gov/products/gao-22-105659.

ABOUT THE EDITORS

Daniel J. Chenok is Executive Director of the IBM Center for The Business of Government, where he oversees all of the Center's activities in connecting research to benefit government. He serves in numerous industry leadership positions, with organizations that include the Partnership for Public Service, the National Academy of Public Administration, and the Senior Executives Association. As a career government executive, Mr. Chenok served as Branch Chief for Information Policy and Technology with the Office of Management and Budget.

Michael J. Keegan is the Leadership Fellow at the IBM Center for The Business of Government and Host of *The Business of Government Hour*. He has interviewed and profiled hundreds of senior government executives and thought leaders who are tackling some of the most significant public management challenges facing government today. He has more than two decades of experience in both the private and public sectors, encompassing strategic planning, business process redesign, performance management, change management, executive and team coaching, and risk-financing.

ABOUT THE CONTRIBUTORS

Jason Briefel is a Partner and Director of Government & Public Affairs at Shaw, Bransford & Roth, P.C., in Washington, D.C.

Ignacio F. Cruz is an Assistant Professor of Communication at Northwestern University. His research focuses on the Future of Work, specifically how organizations strategically design, implement, and assess emerging technologies in their workflows.

Kevin Dehmer is Executive Director of the Heldrich Center for Workforce Development. He is responsible for executive management and day-to-day oversight of research, administration, communications, program development, technical assistance, policy implementation, client services, and project operations.

Ana-Maria Dimand, PhD, is Assistant Professor of Public Policy and Administration School of Public Service at Boise State University. Her research focuses on public management, specifically on issues related to government contracting, collaborative governance, innovation, and sustainability.

Paula Ganga, PhD, is an Assistant Professor of Political Economy at Duke Kunshan University and a Visiting Fellow at Stanford University. She was a Postdoctoral Fellow at Columbia University's Harriman Institute and the Skalny Center for Polish and Central European Studies at the University of Rochester after completing her doctorate at Georgetown University.

Rob Handfield is the Bank of America University Distinguished Professor of Operations and Supply Chain Management, North Carolina State University. In addition to his faculty position, Handfield is Executive Director and founder of the Supply Chain Resource Cooperative, based at Poole College. Handfield is Editor in Chief of the *Logistics* journal. He has published more than 140 peer reviewed publications, authored several books on supply chain management.

Ken Lish is an Audit Director at the National Science Foundation Office of Inspector General in Alexandria, Virginia. Ken is responsible for overseeing NSF's programs, operations, and $35 billion grant portfolio.

Shelley H. Metzenbaum, The BETTER Project (Bringing Everyone Together to Enhance Results), was OMB Associate Director for performance/personnel management, founding President of The Volcker Alliance, and head of EPA Regional Operations & State/Local Relations. She teaches and writes about using goals and data to improve outcomes without making people afraid, compromising performance.

Chris Mihm, PhD, is an Adjunct Professor at Syracuse University, teaching graduate courses on public administration and democracy and performance management. He is the former Managing Director for Strategic Issues at the U.S. Government Accountability Office where he led GAO's work on governance, strategy, and performance issues. He is also a fellow and former Board Chair of the U.S. National Academy of Public Administration.

Renata Miskell is the Deputy Assistant Secretary for Accounting Policy and Financial Transparency, at the U.S. Department of the Treasury, Washington, D.C.

Heath Mitchell supports front office operations for FEMA's Federal Insurance Directorate in Washington, D.C., where he coordinates activities for the High Impact Service: filing a claim under the National Flood Insurance Program. Heath Co-Chairs FEMA's Grassroots Customer Experience Community, which advocates for more FEMA services to embrace principles of human-centered design.

Ilia Murtazashvili, PhD, is Professor of Public Policy and Political Economy and Co-Director of the Center for Governance and Markets at the University of Pittsburgh and a Research Partner with SpectrumX: An NSF Spectrum Innovation Center. At the Center for Governance and Markets, Ilia leads the Research Program on Governance of Emerging Technologies.

Andrea S. Patrucco, PhD, is an Assistant Professor of Supply Chain Management Department of Marketing and Logistics at the College of Business, Florida International University, in Miami, Florida. His research interests are in the field of management of buyer-supplier relationships in both the private and public sectors.

Tony Scott is President and CEO, Intrusion, Inc. Prior to becoming CEO of Intrusion, Inc, Tony founded the TonyScottGroup, a Washington, D.C., and Silicon Valley-based consulting and venture capital firm. During the Obama administration, Tony served as Federal Chief Information Officer, with oversight, budget, and management responsibilities for the more than $85 billion the federal government spends annually on IT. Tony has also served as CIO of Microsoft, CIO of the Walt Disney Company, and CTO of General Motors.

Kayla Schwoerer, PhD, is an Assistant Professor in the Department of Public Administration & Policy at Rockefeller College (University at Albany, SUNY) and an Assistant Professor in the Department of Public Administration and Political Science at Vrije Universiteit (VU) in Amsterdam. Her research focuses broadly on the intersection of public and nonprofit management, science, technology and innovation studies, and social equity.

Stephanie Walsh, PhD, is the Assistant Director of Research at the Heldrich Center for Workforce Development. She earned her doctorate in planning and public policy at Rutgers University. Her research interests focus on how data can inform public programs and policies to better support service delivery and improve individual outcomes.

Michael Windle leads marketing efforts for FEMA's National Flood Insurance Program. He previously served as CX Team Lead in FEMA's Individual Assistance Division, and also worked at OMB leading the Recovering from a Disaster Life Experience effort created by Executive Order 14058. In 2020, Michael founded FEMA's Grassroots Customer Experience Community.

ACKNOWLEDGMENTS

This book commemorates the 25th anniversary of The IBM Center for
The Business of Government. Over the last quarter-century of connecting
research to practice, we have benefited greatly from collaborating with
partners, through various networks and ecosystems, who also find value in
improving the management and operation of government.

The insights and recommendations outlined in this book have been 25
years in the making. We've drawn on the Center's extensive library of over
451 reports, 800 radio show interviews with government leaders and
influencers, and extensive roundtables and other sessions to convene and
collaborate with thought leaders, experts, and government executives who
want to make a difference in shaping the future of government that can best
serve the people. While we cannot acknowledge each individual for their
inspiration, support, and ideas across the years, we would like to thank
those who have worked with the IBM Center in contributing to the ideas
presented here.

To help government leaders build capabilities and resilience to prepare
for future shocks, we launched an initiative in collaboration with the IBM
Institute for Business Value (IBV) and the National Academy for Public
Administration that developed content instrumental to Parts I and II of this
book. Other partners included the Center for American Studies in Rome
and the American Chamber of Commerce in the Netherlands. We would
like to thank all those who participated in the Future Shocks initiative, and
especially those who authored reports and blogs disseminating the insights
of this initiative—specifically, principal author Chris Mihm (former Managing
Director, Strategic Issues, Government Accountability Office), as well as
report authors Professor Robert Handfield (North Carolina State, Pool
College of Management), and Tony Scott (former U.S. OMB Federal Chief
Information Officer).

We would like to acknowledge and thank our IBM colleagues who drafted
content and contributed to the success of the Future Shocks initiative.
They include current global government leaders Cristina Caballe and
Florian Breger, as well as former leaders Mike Stone and Tim Paydos; IBV
leaders Kee Won Song and Dave Zaharchuk, as well as IBV contributors
Gerry Parham, Wendy Roth, Jacob Dencik, Catherine Fillare, and Karen
Butner; and other IBM colleagues including Meeyoung Yoon, Gina Gutierrez,
Maren McKenna, Sharon Moore, and Franciso Pelayo. We would also
like to express our appreciation for another successful collaboration with
the National Academy of Public Administration led by Terry Gerton, Joe
Mitchell, along with Erika Cintron, Jillian McGuffey, and Kyle Romano.

Part III of this book would not have been possible without the thoughtful contributions of our 25th Anniversary Challenge Grant winners: Jason Briefel, Ignacio F. Cruz, Kevin Dehmer, Ana-Maria Dimand, Paula Ganga, Ken Lish, Shelley Metzenbaum, Renata Miskell, Heath Mitchell, Ilia Murtazashvili, Andrea S. Patrucco, Kayla Schwoerer, Stephanie Walsh, and Michael Windle. We truly appreciate colleagues who reviewed portions of this book, offered comments and suggestions, and gave of their time to review and comment on the text. Specifically, we wish to thank James Christian Blockwood, Gabe Chang, Alice Fakir, Leanne Haselden, John Marshall, Emily Tavoulareas, and Dave Wennergren,

This book and the commemoration of our 25th anniversary would not be possible without the support of IBM executives over the years, especially Susan Wedge, who is currently the Managing Partner for the U.S. Public & Federal Market in IBM Consulting. Their continued support has sustained the Center and has made what we do a reality. Special thanks and appreciation go to our IBM Center colleagues Ruth Gordon, Margie Graves, and Mark Newsome. As you can imagine, the Center's success is built on the work and effort of those who have come before, especially former Center Directors Mark Abramson and Jonathan Breul, and Former Center Senior Fellow John Kamensky. We'd also like to acknowledge other colleagues who we have helped the Center meet its missions throughout the years, including Executive Fellow Ed DeSeve, Visiting Fellows Katherine Barrett and Richard Greene, Angela Evans, Danny Harris, and Praja Trivedi, and some 500 authors who have brought forward insights and expertise through Center reports and guest blogs.

Finally, big thanks to Dan Muggeo, Frank Coffy, Anthony Hanna, and Steven Vogel with Daniels+Roberts, Inc., for their exceptional creative, editing, and production assistance. We are grateful for their steady patience and invaluable guidance in the layout and design of this manuscript. Thanks to Jon Sisk and Jaylene Perez, with Rowman & Littlefield Publishers, for their help in publishing the book.

Daniel J. Chenok
Michael J. Keegan

ABOUT THE IBM CENTER FOR
THE BUSINESS OF GOVERNMENT

Founded in 1998, the IBM Center for The Business of Government helps public sector executives improve the effectiveness of government with practical ideas and original thinking. The IBM Center sponsors independent research by top minds in the academic and nonprofit communities. It focuses on the future of the operation and management of the public sector. Since its creation, the IBM Center has published 23 books and nearly 451 reports. All reports and other material are available free of charge at the IBM Center website: https://www.businessofgovernment.org/.

Over the past 25 years, the IBM Center has provided government leaders with instructive ideas that inform actions. Based on this guidance, the IBM Center has earned a reputation for addressing public management issues with a deep understanding—rooted in both theory and practice.

The IBM Center competitively awards stipends to outstanding researchers across the United States and the world. Each award winner is expected to produce a research report on an important management topic.

In addition to its reports and books, the IBM Center publishes *The Business of Government* magazine. The Center also produces *The Business of Government Hour*—an interview program with government executives who are changing the way government does business.

To find out more about the IBM Center and its research stipend program, to review a full list of publications, or to download a report, visit https://www.businessofgovernment.org/.